AVRIL E

SHE'S COMPLICATED

Natasha Jay

TRICKLE
ROCK
BOOKS

© 2005 by Trickle Rock Books Inc.
First printed in 2006 10 9 8 7 6 5 4 3 2 1
Printed in Canada

The Publisher: Trickle Rock Books Inc.

Library and Archives Canada Cataloguing in Publication

Jay, Natasha, 1982–
  Avril Lavigne: she's complicated / Natasha Jay.

Includes bibliographical references.
ISBN-13: 978-1-897206-00-3
ISBN-10: 1-897206-00-3

  1. Lavigne, Avril. 2. Rock musicians—Canada—
Biography. 3. Singers—Canada—Biography. I. Title.

ML420.L412J42 2006   782.42166'092   C2006-902540-1

Cover Image: Courtesy of Shayne Robinson/WireImage.com

Photo Credits: Every effort has been made to accurately credit the sources of photographs. Any errors or omissions should be directed to the publisher for changes in future editions. Photographs courtesy of International Communications Systems (title page); Shayne Robinson/WireImage.com (p. 121).

PC: P5

contents

Dedication

To all the ordinary girls who ever dreamed
of being extraordinary.

Acknowledgements

Special thanks to my publisher and to Mark Jowett.

introduction

When I began writing this book, I thought of my own singing debut: I was two years old, and I was at an Amway convention with my parents. I couldn't fall asleep in the daycare and demanded that I be taken to my parents, who were in a massive hall that was packed with people for the concluding gala. As I sat on my mother's lap, I watched a little girl (probably three times my age) go up on stage and sing "Bah Bah Black Sheep," and I thought to myself, "I can do that." Next thing I knew, I was off, heading with great intent towards the stage. My mother, who was busy speaking to the people next to her, got the fright of her life when she looked in the direction of the stage and realized that her two-year-old daughter was up there, microphone in hand, singing "Rock-A-Bye Baby" in front of a crowd of 2000. Subsequently, my mother ran up on stage to join me and sing along (something for which I have never forgiven her), and so began my life as a musician.

The rest of my story of classical training, competitions and university may differ from that of other musicians, but I am certain that each musician's career begins with a story such as this: a tale of unintentional risk (for we did not realize it was a risk at the time) that showed us and our families that we felt at home on stage; something in our genes told us that we were meant to be musicians.

Whereas some musicians are content to maintain music as their hobby, playing regularly with friends and at open-mike sessions, others yearn for bigger and better things. But making a career solely as a musician takes more than just talent: it is a sound, a look and a certain *je ne sais quoi* (more commonly known as the "X-factor") that make up the frontrunners in the recording industry of today. This triple threat, combined with a case of "being in the right place at the right time," along with the help of a well-oiled marketing machine, spells success for many of the biggest stars in the business. In 2002 this formula proved its legitimacy with the emergence of the explosive pop-rock empire of Canadian-born Avril Lavigne.

The first time I heard Avril Lavigne sing was at a summer job. At any of the jobs I have ever held, I have always insisted on having a radio on my desk so I can listen to music while I work, and this job was no exception. One day I found myself singing along to a catchy tune, sung by an edgy girl who sounded as though she wouldn't take any crap from anyone. Something was different about this girl. When I heard that she was Canadian, I felt extremely patriotic, of course, and thought it my duty to introduce her to the rest of world.

Although I was supposed to be working, I decided to write to Rick Dees (radio host of Rick Dees and the Weekly Top 40) and tell him about this talented Canadian, Avril Lavigne, and her stellar hit "Complicated." I recommended that he add her to his countdown as quickly as possible and informed him of what a big hit she was going to be. Well, as smart as I thought I was, I have a feeling that Ms. Lavigne's label, Arista Records, had already beat me to it (who would have thought…), as the song entered the charts the following week.

Since 2002, Avril Lavigne's career has skyrocketed to heights I'm sure she could not have imagined in her wildest dreams. Two internationally successful Number One albums later, and on the verge of a promising acting and modeling career, this multi-talented firecracker appears to be just getting started, and I am ecstatic at the opportunity to document her life and times so far. Unfortunately, because of her thus-far brief career, little has been written about the singer-songwriter. Rummaging through dozens of archived magazines and online sources, I wondered how I would bring it all together. However, after a couple of weeks of reading everything I could find about Avril Lavigne, my ideas started to take shape.

Although this book follows the path of one gifted musician, I hope you will also learn something about the current music business and how a young, spunky girl like Avril Lavigne can thrive in such a cutthroat industry. With a great deal of research and the help of a personal interview with a highly esteemed record executive, who was generous enough to offer his time and memories, I hope you will discover, as I did, the fascinating story of a truly unique human being and the creation of an unlikely star.

a star is born

When John and Judy Lavigne gave birth to Avril Ramona Lavigne in Belleville, Ontario, on September 27, 1984, no one had any idea that a star had just been born. When the family moved 25 miles up the hill to Napanee five years later, they also had no idea of the impact Avril would have on the reputation of the tiny town. There was no way that anyone could have guessed that, from a town where not a single record shop is found, such a musical talent could emerge. It was impossible to know that the quiet streets of Napanee could produce the leader of a pop-rocking, skateboarding, boot-stomping, baggy pants–wearing rebellion: a movement among youth that would change the face of music for the generation to come.

"It starts out dark, the lights come on and then there's, like, thousands of people watching me. All I ever thought about when I was younger was that's the kind of crowd I always wanted." There was one person who always knew the destiny of this diminutive girl: Avril Lavigne herself.

The one thing that was obvious to the Lavignes and the community of Napanee was that Avril Lavigne could sing. Belting out tunes at home since the age of two, her love for music was evident from the get-go. However, the music that she encountered at her beginnings was a far cry from the rebellious rock star persona of her current music career.

With a desire to get Avril singing in public, her mother convinced her church to form a choir, which performed twice a week. French-born John Lavigne, who worked as a technician for the telephone company, Bell Canada, and Judy Lavigne, a full-time mother, attended church regularly and were accompanied by Avril and their two other children, Matt (born in 1982) and

Michelle (born in 1987). Judy Lavigne, who realized the potential in her daughter's talent, soon persuaded the choral director to give Avril a solo. And so, in one of her first public solo performances, a very accomplished 10-year-old Avril sang the beautiful hymn "Near to the Heart of God," written by Cleland McAfee, at the church's Christmas celebration. Even back then Avril showed some of her now infamous attitude, as John Lavigne recalls, "She hogged the mike."

Of course, Avril is not the first famous singer to begin her vocal career in church. Jessica Simpson, Usher, Britney Spears, Beyoncé Knowles and Kelly Clarkson, among others, all had their start with their local church choirs. However, it is much easier to see the gospel influence in these R&B/pop singers' music than in Avril Lavigne's raging, rock-driven pop anthems. So where did this harder edge come from?

Well, it definitely wasn't from the town of Napanee. With a population of approximately 5000, Napanee appears to be a charming place to grow up in, with its main street described as "remarkably well preserved, with Victorian facades occupied by mom-and-pop shops." Although its largest industry is Goodyear Tires, Napanee is largely known as a farming community, and it houses a top-quality horse sales and leasing company, Garrison Equine, which "offers a wide range of horses and ponies to fit most budgets, from the backyard enthusiast to the 'A' level competitor." Sounds

AvRiL tRiViA

Avril's favorite pizza joint in Napanee is La Pizzeria, claiming to be the "home of Avril Lavigne's favorite pizza," which contains green olives, pepperoni and mushrooms. Unfortunately for La Pizzeria, Avril is now a vegetarian and doesn't eat mushrooms or pepperoni anymore.

like the perfect setup for a future country music star, as that is, believably, the kind of music that dominates the airwaves throughout the small town.

It is not hard to imagine, then, that besides church music, country music was Avril Lavigne's first major influence as a singer. In fact, many of her idols while growing up were country singers, such as Canada's own Shania Twain, the Dixie Chicks, Faith Hill and Garth Brooks. At a time when country was not the most popular form of music, these artists were able to revolutionize the genre and bring it into the mainstream during the '90s, accomplishing record-breaking sales. Young musicians like Avril Lavigne, who grew up watching and listening to these artists, were the beneficiaries of their legacy. Many of Avril's first public appearances were at talent competitions at local country fairs, where she sang karaoke-style to backtracks and reveled in the applause of her friends and family. Eventually she began to win some of these contests, forecasting the unreal success that was to come to her in the years ahead.

One contest in particular was a turning point in Avril's chosen path. In 1999, at only 14, she heard about a radio contest with a prize of joining one of her biggest influences, Shania Twain, on stage at the Corel Centre (now called Scotiabank Place) in Ottawa. Not wasting a minute, Lavigne recorded herself singing a track from Twain's first album and sent it in. She won the contest and was flown to Ottawa, where she performed a duet of "What Made You Say That?" with Shania Twain.

You would think that performing on stage with one of your idols, who also happens to be the biggest sensation in country music, would cause a little bit of stage fright for a 14-year-old girl. Not only that, but the venue was not quite the country-fair audience that she was used to, with a sold-out crowd of 20,000. However, as Avril explains to *Chart* magazine, "Before I went on everyone kept asking me, 'Are you nervous? Are you nervous? Are you going to be okay?' And I kept telling everyone, 'I'm fine! What are you talking about?' So I walked up on stage, sang the song, walked off and said, 'Yep, this is what I want to do for the rest of my life.' I never felt so happy."

Apparently, she also made this goal quite clear to her duet partner, telling Shania Twain that she planned on being a famous singer one day. Years later, when Shania Twain appeared on *Much Music*, the host played a pre-recorded message from a mystery fan that said: "Do you remember me? I sang in Ottawa at the Corel Centre with you. We sang 'What Made You Say That?'"

> Shania did remember but confessed that she had not believed her friends and family when they told her so many times that the young, fuzzy-haired girl she had shared her stage with back then was the same girl who now rocked stages all around the world. Now that she knew, Shania promised to send Avril a video of their duet.

After her amazing encounter with Shania Twain, Avril could barely contain herself, saying, "I'd never smiled so much in my life—it was like perma-smile." This experience now gave Avril a concrete goal to work towards and the motivation to do it. "I thought, 'This is what I'm going to do with my life, walk out on stage, have my own band, and be doing my own concert with my own songs.' I'm serious—this was meant to happen to me."

chapter two

the makings of a pop-rock rebel

A girl who sang church hymns and country music doesn't sound much like the rock goddess we have come to love, does it? So how did this country-singing, church-going young girl develop into the star we all know today?

Avril's first exposure to any kind of alternative music came from her brother's CD collection, when she would listen to one of her future favorites, the Goo Goo Dolls. Even now, she still listens to their music and praises them every chance she gets: "I love the Goo Goo Dolls. When I sit there and listen to their CD, it really touches me and reminds me why I do what I'm doing. I'm like, 'Oh my god, I'm so lucky to be doing what I'm doing.'" Truthfully, the CD was one of very few alternatives to country music that Avril Lavigne listened to while growing up in Napanee.

If you were to ask Avril what there is to do in her hometown, you would probably get a big fat "nothing" for an answer. The lack of things to do is one reason that music became such a big part of her life from an early age, as kids were often forced to entertain themselves in their scenic, yet rather unexciting, small town. With the rocker attitude already in her blood, Avril also was grounded a great deal of the time because of various misbehaviors (such as sneaking out of the house!), and music was her source of amusement while stuck in her room at home or at school.

Although she was disgruntled at being grounded, the time Avril spent alone in her room proved to be an invaluable part of her development as a musician. Bored and locked in her house for hours at a time, she picked up her dad's acoustic guitar and taught herself how to play. She practiced Lenny Kravitz's "Fly Away" over

AvRiL tRiViA

Avril follows a vegan diet 90% of the time
and loves eating pasta.

and over again until her teeny hands could play the chord structure. Who knew that being bored and grounded could turn you into a superstar?

Avril also kept herself busy with activities other than music. Admittedly a tomboy, she preferred to hang out with the guys rather than the girls, as her interests seemed to coincide better with them. As a child, Avril looked up to her brother Matt quite a bit and enjoyed going camping, hunting and fishing with him. She was also into dirt biking and went on canoe trips with her family.

Not as interested in makeup and fashion as were other girls her age, Avril would rather watch sports on TV with the guys and was also a talented athlete herself. She participated in soccer, basketball, waterskiing and track and field, even setting a triple-jump record in her school track meet in 1998. She played baseball in the summer and, apparently, was not a bad pitcher.

In the winter she was quite a skilled hockey player, playing both right wing and center positions on an all-boys team, and won the MVP award for two years running. It also turns out that she was a bit of a scrapper on the ice, as she recalls a fight she once had with the opposing goalie: "One time I beat up a goalie. My dad has that on video. The guy took his glove and smacked me, and I was like, 'Whoa!' I pushed him into the net, he punched me, I punched him. It was awesome."

Her dad remembers another time when it wasn't so much of a retaliation: "One time…the two teams were coming off the ice, and next thing you know there's a great big commotion, and moms and dads were pulling kids out. I went to the dressing room thinking, 'Who's that rotten kid that started this?' and turns out some guy called one of Avril's teammates fat pig or something, and Avril slugged him right in the mask. So she started it."

As many of her fans know, Avril was also an avid skateboarder. She learned to skate in Grade 10 at Napanee's skatepark but admits that her skills have gone downhill because she is so busy recording and touring and does not get to practice as much anymore. Avril's parents always encouraged her to get involved in activities with her friends, but John Lavigne is the first to admit that he was not a fan of the "Sk8er" boyfriends she brought home as a result of this particular interest: "I didn't like them much," he says.

Like most kids, a lot of Avril's time was taken up by school. She started at Westdale Public School but was forced to transfer because she was being bullied. She was much more successful after she transferred to Cornerstone Christian Academy, a private Christian school. Cornerstone allowed Avril to excel in what she did best. She participated in plays and was musically involved in school activities. When she graduated, the school awarded Avril the Marie Cowling Memorial Award for her musical achievements.

> Avril describes herself as being a "hyper kid" and was usually looking for attention. "I'd be doing cartwheels, going, 'Everybody look at me! Watch this! Watch this!'...just this annoying little kid bouncing off the walls."

She went on to attend the Napanee District Secondary School, where things did not sail along quite as smoothly for her. In high school there is a natural separation of students into various social groups (jocks, preps, goths, etc.), and Avril connected immediately with the skaters. However, because she was not like most of the girls her age, she found high school to be an unwelcoming place. "School gave me an inferiority complex...I never did my work, was always talking and failed all my tests because I didn't try," she explains.

Avril is remembered by some of her teachers as being a friendly, focused and polite student, but she also displayed some early rock star behavior, which got her into trouble on countless occasions. She was suspended and kicked out of her classes for talking or for not completing homework assignments. So, even though she was bright, and probably just as (or maybe even more) intelligent as the majority of students in her grade, Avril was already developing into quite a unique being and did not find her studies at Napanee District Secondary an easy time.

However, what she *did* learn while growing up in Napanee that would help her oncoming career was stage presence. Besides singing at country fairs, Avril sang at any place in her small town where she could find a willing audience, including at hockey games, at a Canadian Tire celebration and even at an insurance company Christmas party.

AvRiL tRiViA

If she hadn't become a famous singer, Avril considered becoming a police officer when she was younger.

Avril also joined the local theater company, Lennox Community Theatre, at the age of 11. The company, which produces plays and musicals for the surrounding community, puts on around five productions per year. Lavigne, who appeared in three of these shows, was welcomed by the theater's director, Tim Picotte, who said that "Avril has always had the sparkle, she's got showmanship."

At only 12 years old, Avril was cast as Sally in the production of *You're a Good Man Charlie Brown*, for which she spent hours perfecting an exact imitation of the character's hairstyle. Foreshadowing her near future, she also played a rebellious teenager in the production of *Godspell* a few years later. Can you believe that Avril actually resisted the outrageous costuming that Picotte proposed she wear as she was not comfortable wearing punk clothing? Funny how things change.

It was her involvement in the Lennox Community Theatre that landed Avril her first recording gig. Local folksinger and songwriter Steve Medd, who happened to be a friend of Avril's father and was currently gearing up to record his own independent album, saw Lavigne on stage at the theater and thought her voice would match some of the ideas he had for his songs. After Medd talked with Avril and her family and played her some samples of his work, it was agreed that Avril would sing on his album at a recording studio in the nearby town of Kingston.

And so, at only 14 years of age, Avril Lavigne walked into a recording studio for the first time and formed an instant connection with the process, recording her part in just one take! Blown away by Avril's first attempt at recording, Steve Medd tells Star-tv.com, "She walks into the studio and bang, she nails it. This is a girl that seemed to have no fear and…you could tell this is truly what she loved to do. This is a girl that was born to sing."

Avril sang in three songs on the album titled *Quinte Spirit*: "Touch the Sky," "World to Me" and the title track "The Quinte Spirit." Medd also called on Lavigne one year later when he recorded *My Window to You*, a tribute album to poet E. Pauline Johnson, on which Avril contributed to "Two Rivers" and "Temple of Life." Medd indicates that Avril was very mature for her age and very focused when it came to getting down to business in the studio. He also recalls that she was extremely enjoyable to work with, had an engaging personality and was very kind-hearted, having babysat both his kids. "They will say to this day that she is the best babysitter we ever had," Medd says.

Not only did the project give Avril the amazing experience of working in a studio for the first time, but it also provided her first taste of music for charity as half of the proceeds from Medd's CD sales and MP3 downloads went towards the production of the *Quinte Spirit Music Festival*, where Avril performed in 1998. The festival, which Medd explained is meant to "inspire musical and artistic creativity in the Napanee-Quinte region," is a popular local event that showcases up-and-coming talent from the Greater Napanee area.

A release party for *Quinte Spirit* was held at the local Chapters bookstore in Kingston, where a few of the contributors from the album, including Avril Lavigne, performed for their community. Little did she know that there was a man in the audience watching her that day who would give her a ticket out of Napanee to begin her life as an internationally renowned rock star.

"nettwerking"

The man who was watching from the audience that day in Kingston was none other than Cliff Fabri, who would eventually become Avril's first manager. Fabri ran a company out of Kingston called RomanLine Productions, and he saw something special in Lavigne right away. He realized first of all what an amazing voice she had and that, at only fve feet tall, with delicate and petite facial features, she also had a unique air to her that was certainly pleasant to look at. However, it was Avril's attitude that struck Fabri as something that set her apart from the other performers that day.

Fabri shares a story about Avril that helps explain what he saw in her: "She goes hunting all the time with her brother and dad. Here's this sweet little thing, and I said to her one time, 'What about when a little doe comes out and starts nudging up to the mother? What do you do?' And she goes [making the sound of a shotgun blast] 'Dinner.' I was like, yeah! I loved the toughness."

Fabri had worked with several artists already and was well versed in what it took to get a record deal in the works. He also understood the importance of getting as much exposure and live practice as possible, so he arranged as many public appearances for Lavigne as he could, in Kingston, Napanee and their surrounding areas

But most of all, he realized that Avril had the potential to be very different from the current superstars in the industry—namely, many of the boy bands and acts such as Britney Spears—whose image was almost fabricated, with pre-written material appearing on all their albums. Fabri saw room in the industry for self-made musicians and, consequently, encouraged Avril to continue her efforts in writing original material. She worked on polishing her songwriting abilities, though her live performance sets still remained full of cover tunes, mainly country music.

AvRiL tRiViA

Some of Avril's songs are featured in the
PlayStation *Karaoke* games.

Although Avril was a pretty girl, and admittedly a tomboy, at 14 years of age her looks were rather nondescript. Like most young teenagers, she seemed uncomfortable in her skin and unsure of her personal style. She had short, fuzzy hair, which she occasionally braided when it grew long enough to do so. She also wore glasses and little to no makeup. While Fabri was aware that a more refined image would benefit the young singer, he also knew that Avril's talent was the most important element to nurture at the moment. He was confident that her physical style would evolve in time as she began to develop more as a recording artist.

Fabri set about doing what managers do best: he put his plan to promote his new prodigy into action. The first step of the plan was to get some kind of recording together that would showcase Avril's talent. Most people probably think this would involve going into the studio, laying down some tracks with a producer and coming out with a three- or four-song demo that sounded reasonably professional. But Fabri had other ideas and, because he was on a limited budget, he made a simple video recording of her singing in her father's garage.

In the music industry, a common phrase is "being in the right place at the right time." Similarly, whether you have a professional demo or not, you must know the right people to give your demo to—people who will actually listen to it (much harder than it sounds!). Luckily, Fabri did know the right people. Because he had been in the business for quite a while, he had gained the contacts that would prove extremely valuable to Avril Lavigne's career.

The first interest in Avril came from Brian Hetherman, who worked for Universal Music in Toronto. Although he did not sign her after his trip to Napanee to meet her, Hetherman sent her a package of CDs to encourage her to expand her musical knowledge. Listening to the CDs was Avril's first rock experience with anything other than the Goo Goo Dolls, as the collection included albums from artists like Blink-182. Fascinated, she ran to the nearest record store and began to broaden her previously sheltered musical existence with bands such as Matchbox 20 and Third Eye Blind. Avril's eyes began to widen, and she was starting to get an idea of how she wanted her own music to sound.

Another contact that Fabri had was with Nettwerk Records. As Canada's largest independently owned record label and management company, Nettwerk manages many of the industry's biggest artists, including Sarah McLachlan, Dido and the Barenaked Ladies. Although they have offices around the world, in New York, London and Los Angeles, Nettwerk's head office is based in Vancouver, British Columbia, where cofounders Terry McBride and Mark Jowett reside.

Nettwerk was originally founded in 1984 in support of Jowett's band, Moev, which McBride managed, after the label to which it was signed went bankrupt. Since then, Nettwerk has become a powerhouse in the music industry, housing not only the Nettwerk label and management departments but also Nettwerk One (its publishing offices), Artwerks (a graphic design company), NuTone (an electronic music label) and The Sync (an "interactive Arts Venue, Shop and Music Lounge"), and it is affiliated with a variety of other industry-related companies. Terry McBride is now the CEO of the company and a well-respected industry guru. Mark Jowett acts as vice-president of the company and heads the Artist and Repertoire Department (more commonly referred to as "A&R," the department is responsible for acquiring new talent for the label, similar to a talent scout), and he is also an esteemed member of the industry.

Because he had managed another artist who was signed to the Nettwerk label, Cliff Fabri was well acquainted with the staff there. After recording young Avril, Fabri made sure that he placed the tape in the hands of the Nettwerk executive, Mark Jowett. In a personal interview, Jowett recalls his first impression of Avril Lavigne and her music when he watched the tape of her singing in her father's garage: "I was really impressed by her persona at the time, just watching the video, she had this real kind of ease and glow when she performed, and so she was just an absolute natural." Intrigued by the amazing aura that this diminutive girl exuded, Jowett agreed to meet with her.

Fabri and the Lavignes headed to Toronto for a well-known Music and Film Conference and Festival called North By Northeast. The conference, which has taken place since 1994, is open to anyone who can afford to attend (delegate passes range from $100 to $300) and allows up-and-coming new artists to learn from, and hobnob with, some of the industry's top guns. Mirrored in Austin, Texas, by a similar event called South By Southwest, the festival portions have given starts to many of today's bigger artists, such as Feist, Sam Roberts, the Fugees, Norah Jones and Franz Ferdinand.

The conference is also a place where A&R representatives arrange meetings to discuss potentially signing a new artist. It was at

North By Northeast where Avril Lavigne and her parents first met with Mark Jowett to discuss Avril's future. Sitting outside at a coffee house in Toronto, Jowett described the teenager as being "quite shy…she had her hair in braids, she was very pretty…she seemed really quite special." Although he was not entirely ready to offer her a recording contract, he expressed an interest in helping to facilitate a demo recording so that Avril could realize some of her own material while working with others in the industry.

When he returned to his Vancouver office, Jowett arranged a trip for Avril to visit New York, a city where she could work with more established songwriters and develop her writing skills. During her stay in New York, she spent a great deal of time with Peter Zizzo, a talented songwriter and producer with whom Nettwerk had a good relationship. Zizzo had worked with artists such as Jennifer Lopez, Céline Dion and Vanessa Carlton, and Jowett thought that Zizzo was the right person to help guide Avril in advancing her own songwriting skills.

As her exposure to music was rather limited, and she was only just beginning to open up to new styles, Lavigne was unsure of the kind of music she wanted to produce. Jowett thought that working with Peter Zizzo might help to clarify things a little.

He joined Peter and Avril in New York at one point and remembers sitting at a restaurant with them on Broadway (one of the most famous theater locations in the world) as Avril expressed how excited she was to be there. When she left to go home, she could not wait to return to New York as quickly as possible. Her wish would be granted, and very soon.

biting the big apple

Trips to New York started to become a regular occurrence for Avril. Through his extensive connections, Cliff Fabri arranged for Avril to meet with Ken Krongard, an A&R rep from Arista Records, during one of her visits to New York. Arista, which has morphed many times—and continues to, merging with J Records in August 2005—is an independent label distributed through Sony/BMG, which accommodates one of the most diverse groups of artists in the industry, from Outkast to Dido to Carrie Underwood to the Eurythmics.

At the time of Avril's meeting with Krongard, Arista had just signed an artist by the name of Pink, a spunky R&B rocker who certainly did her own thing. Like Avril, Pink was determined not to be grouped with the many manufactured, pretty-girl pop stars who were topping the charts. Instead, she wanted to rise above that crowd by being herself and writing her own material. This knowledge was comforting to Avril when Arista showed interest in signing her to the label. As soon as Krongard heard Avril's voice and saw her potential, he knew that this girl had a gift that would make her a valuable asset to the Arista roster. Krongard contacted his boss to give him the news and asked Avril to prepare a showcase, which she would perform privately for him on her next visit to New York.

Krongard's boss, who was none other than Antonio "L.A." Reid, and president of the label at the time, was extremely well known. He was responsible for launching the careers of such internationally successful acts as TLC, Usher, Dido and Pink. Reid was a big name and one of the most influential moguls in the music industry—performing for him was the opportunity of a lifetime for Avril. While the people around her were in a frenzy, frantically advising her to stay calm and not be nervous, Avril was not worried

AvRiL tRiViA

At 18 years and 4 months, Avril held the number two spot in the U.K. for the youngest soloist to have an album at number one (behind 12-year-old Neil Reid, in 1972).

at all. Blissfully unaware of Reid's importance and the complexities and politics of the recording industry, Avril knew exactly what she had to do. "All I knew was that if I sang for this guy and if he liked me, that would make me able to get a record and that's all I wanted. Basically I wanted my CD," she explains.

Avril worked with Peter Zizzo to prepare three songs for her showcase, two of his compositions and a song called "Why," which resulted from their collaboration during Avril's first visit to New York. Blown away by the strength in her voice, her naturalness as a performer and the energy that she exuded on stage, Reid was delighted by her showcase. After thanking her politely and telling her how fantastic she had been, he left without another word.

Unsure of the results of the meeting, Lavigne waited anxiously until a limo showed up at the studio, not long after Reid had left the building, and took her and Fabri to the World Trade Center for dinner. Reid was waiting for them there, and he offered Avril a record deal for two albums, along with a publishing advance that satisfied Fabri's prediction that she would be "a millionaire before she sold her first record."

Acknowledging the unlikelihood of her story, Avril is aware of how fortunate she was to land such a deal. "I wasn't even shopping for a deal! That doesn't happen very often. I mean, sometimes bands take 10 years to get a deal! So I was very, very, very lucky." No kidding.

Avril happily accepted the deal but, because she was currently creating a demo for Nettwerk Records, this posed a bit of a dilemma for Mark Jowett. However, as Nettwerk already managed certain artists signed to the Arista label, Jowett and his team respected Lavigne's decision to sign with Reid's label. "We also have Sarah McLachlan and Dido with Arista, and we have a very good relationship with them. So we felt at the time that we should probably let it go, rather than contest that," he explains.

Trusting Lavigne's choice and ultimately encouraging her to move ahead with Arista would, in the end, prove to be a smart choice on the part of Nettwerk Records, as Avril kept their kindness and support in the back of her mind for future use.

start spreading the news, i'm leaving today

The Lavigne family was ecstatic over Arista's offer to invest in their daughter's music career, but Avril faced a major decision regarding her enrollment at Napanee District Secondary School. Recording her debut album would be a full-time commitment and not one that could be fulfilled while living in Napanee. There would be little time for anything extra, including schoolwork. Having never truly fit in or excelled as a high school student, Avril opted not to finish her high school education. She knew that music was what made her feel at home and that is how she wanted to spend the rest of her life. Although she appreciates the importance of getting an education, and still encourages others to pursue their studies, she recognized at a young age that it was not the path for her.

Kerry Stewart, who was the principal at Napanee District Secondary School at the time, understood her decision, stating, "For Avril, her path is quite unique, and she has been successful despite the fact that she hasn't yet completed high school." When it came down to it, Avril knew where she belonged, and when faced with this decision, she only took one thing into consideration: "I wasn't going to turn it down…It's been my dream all my life."

Even though her very religious parents were not overly psyched by her choice to drop out of high school, they understood that Avril's passion for music and performing meant more to their daughter than anything else, and they eventually came around to the idea. Finally, in full support of Avril's new life, John and Judy Lavigne knew that she would get a different kind of education as a musician.

They also realize that without the success and responsibility that her career in music has brought, their daughter would be getting into more trouble: "She can stir the pot if she wants to. If she didn't have this [career] she'd be in more trouble than you can shake a stick at." Remembering the difficulties she had experienced at Napanee Secondary, Avril's parents felt that she had a much better chance of excelling in the music industry. Her fans are probably glad she went for the record deal over her high school diploma!

At the same time as Avril's parents gave their blessing regarding her decision to leave school, they also had to get used to the idea of their 16-year-old moving to New York. Not only did Avril score a sweet record deal, but she was also given access to a beautiful apartment in Greenwich Village. This happening area of New York City, which is close to the theaters of Broadway, has been a Mecca for musicians and other creative types for over 100 years. Although Greenwich is much too expensive for most starving artists to live in these days, it remains a major cultural district in the city.

Now far from a "starving artist" with her multimillion-dollar record deal, Lavigne was comfortably set up in the lush residence Arista had provided. However, because Avril was only 16, the Lavignes sent her older brother, Matt, along to live with her in New York. Matt himself was only in his late teens at the time, but being with Avril put their parents' minds at ease. And of course, it would also be an experience of a lifetime for him to accompany his sister to live in luxury accommodation on Horatio Street in the Village.

Happy with her decision to leave Napanee and excited by the prospects that lay ahead of her, Avril set off with her brother to one of the most musically prosperous cities in the world to begin work on her debut album. The apartment that awaited the two of them was Avril's home for the next four months, and it would, unbeknownst to her, prove to be a frustrating time for the young Canadian songwriter.

Like anyone who moves to a new city, making friends can be difficult, especially when you are 16 years old and not enrolled in high school. Although she had Matt around for support and welcome company, Avril mixed mainly with industry members, who were all much older than her. As she was rather mature for her age, she had no problem holding her own in adult company, but she still craved the companionship of kids her own age. When Matt was out, Avril became rather lonely, being stuck in her Greenwich Village apartment with only her music for company.

Not only was she starved for a bit of teenage fun, but her musical efforts also did not pan out exactly as she had imagined. Arista was not yet aware that Avril was a maturing songwriter in her own right and, consequently, sent her material that was written by more-established industry songwriters. Arista was also under the impression that she was signed as a singer of the "new country" style (which was strongly suggested in her showcase), so the songs they sent Avril did not complement her currently growing interest in other, harder-edged genres of music, such as rock and punk. In New York City, she worked with many skilled writers and even recorded several tracks, but she was just not content with the results of these attempts. She felt that she had something more to say and that the words of others were simply not fulfilling her desire to express herself.

Although she became discouraged, Avril never threw in the towel on the project. This is what she wanted to do; she just had to find a way of doing it that worked for her. She talked about her experience in New York on *Entertainment Tonight*: "I started working with these really talented people, but I just wasn't feeling it; the songs weren't representative of me. I had to write myself. I had to do my music. It was a really stressful time, but I never considered giving up."

And so, after months of hard work in New York, which seemed only to be heading for a dead end, Avril had to figure out how to get her team at Arista to come around to the idea of her putting her own material on the album. She went straight to L.A. Reid himself, and though she had to go through a few people to get to him, Reid was happy to discuss her growing concerns about the direction of the album. He had such great confidence in her abilities that he was willing to let the future starlet figure things out in her own time.

Because the media have often criticized recording companies for forcing their songs on young up-and-comers, Avril set the record straight on what happened in her particular situation: "I got signed so quickly, and because I was young, of course they were going to give me songs to record…Everyone makes it sound like L.A. Reid was giving me all these songs and they weren't gonna let me write and then I got to…It wasn't like that at all." And so, with Reid's blessing, Avril knew it was time to make a drastic change in order to keep her dream of making an album alive and kicking.

the big orange

Satisfied with L.A. Reid's advice to take her time in finding her sound, Lavigne decided that New York was not the place that allowed her to realize her creative destiny. For the first time in her life she opted to move out West, to Los Angeles, where she could find a new environment, new people and a new beginning. This turned out to be a positive move for Avril, as Arista hooked her up with several songwriters who appeared to have a much better grasp of her intentions for her album. Now 3000 miles away from her Greenwich Village apartment, she met up with a seasoned veteran in the songwriting world, Mr. Clif Magness.

Magness maintains a stellar resumé of collaborations, having worked with artists such as Chantal Kreviazuk, Lisa Marie Presley, Billy Idol and Quincy Jones. He first made an impression in the music industry in the 1980s, working on the number one hit "All I Need" with Jack Wagner and "Impulsive" with the popular group Wilson Phillips. Magness won a Grammy for Best Instrumental Arrangement Accompanying Vocal(s) in 1990 for Quincy Jones' "The Places You Find Love" and was also nominated for an Oscar and a Golden Globe for the song "The Day I Fall In Love," from the *Beethoven's 2nd* (1993) movie soundtrack. Magness continued to work with many esteemed performers throughout the 1990s, such as Céline Dion, Hanson, and Amy Grant.

Now he was working with Avril Lavigne, and his diverse past was just what Lavigne needed to get her songwriting going at warp speed. The chemistry was immediate between the two as Magness quickly understood the kind of music that she was trying to get out. He used his experience to bring the yearning songwriter out of the Canadian teenager and make it happen—and fast. During their very first writing session, Avril and Clif wrote the track

"Unwanted" in its entirety, which was later featured on her debut album. After a series of more than a dozen disappointments while in New York, Avril was elated by the successful collaboration and was eager to work with Magness some more. "I was like, 'Yeah! I've found my guy!' We totally clicked, because he just let me guide; he really understood me and let me do my thing."

The two continued to work together, successfully spewing out song after song, five of which ended up on the album, including the album's fourth single, "Losing Grip." Both "Unwanted" and "Losing Grip" had harsh guitars and a definite dark feeling to them, and Lavigne realized that the two songs scared Arista a little. "Arista was drop-dead...afraid that I would come out with a whole album that sounded like 'Unwanted' and 'Losing Grip,'" she said. "I swear they wanted to drop me or something."

Apparently she would have liked this sound to pervade the whole album but understood that in order for her album to thrive in the current music scene, she needed more pop in the mix. Obviously wary of the direction of the album, Arista was relieved to hear this and set the singer up with yet another group of experienced songwriters. This time it was the renowned writing team known as "The Matrix."

The Matrix team consists of St. Louis-born Scott Spock, Lauren Christy, and her Scottish husband, Graham Edwards. Christy, who originates from the United Kingdom, was a semi-successful musician herself as Reptile Susie, the female lead of the all-male band Pink Ash. In 1999, she was dropped from her label, Mercury Records, and decided to give up her dream of becoming a singing

AvRiL tRiViA
Justin Timberlake has admitted to being
a big fan of Avril's.

superstar. At the same time, Spock and Edwards, who were currently in a moderately successful band called DollsHead, had also been recently dropped by Refuge/MCA Records, and they came to a similar conclusion. When the three of them received a request to write a song for an Australian act by the name of Jackson Mendoza, they thought they would give it a try. A week later they wrote yet another song for Christina Aguilera and decided to form The Matrix to help write and produce for other up-and-coming singers.

After working together for many years, The Matrix has had songwriting and producing gigs with a huge number of successful acts, including the Backstreet Boys, Britney Spears, Ricky Martin and Liz Phair. Avril was aware that she needed a slightly more bubblegum sound for her album to be more accessible to the mainstream, so she knew she was in the right place and was excited about joining forces with the team.

Her connection with the songwriting team seemed to be present from the outset, as it had been with Magness, but first they had to overcome a slight bump in the road. Initially under the impression that Lavigne was to be a "Faith Hill" type singer, The Matrix came up with a song that bordered on new country and played it for her and Fabri. "She was a disgruntled little 16 year old who sat and sulked, basically said, 'I don't want to do that kind of stuff,'" recalls Edwards.

Avril was not willing to completely give up on the edgy sound that she had worked so hard to discover with Magness. Thankfully, The Matrix was patient with her and asked Lavigne what she wanted to do. She replied, "I'm 16. I want to rock out." And so, even though Lavigne and Fabri were not too keen on some of the original ideas that The Matrix had come up with prior to her arrival, the team returned to the drawing board and soon understood what she meant after they heard the recording of "Unwanted," which she had made with Clif Magness.

Subsequently, Avril and The Matrix got to work right away and, within hours, arrived at what turned out to be the album's first single, "Complicated." Avril remembers the fateful afternoon in the studio with The Matrix: "Graham sat down with the guitar and was, like, 'Listen to this little idea I have,' and I was like, 'Oh cool,' and then me and Lauren started singing to it. And we just recorded the guitar part and then went and [lay] on a blanket in the sun and wrote lyrics to it, Lauren and I."

Turning out song after song was a great writing experience for both Avril and The Matrix team, resulting in five of the songs being put on the debut album. Three of the songs, namely "Complicated," "Sk8r Boi" and "I'm With You," became the first three singles from the album and were all Number One hits. Talk about a winning collaboration!

Not only did the personalities click on this partnership, the atmosphere that surrounded Lavigne was also geared towards success. Now many miles away from her home, and also her first time being completely away from her family, she became reflective about her life and experiences, which gave her plenty of ideas to fuel her songwriting ventures with The Matrix. Avril also found the city of Los Angeles fascinating. It was full of things she had never seen before, either in the tiny town of Napanee or in New York. Inspired by California's lush scenery, she remembers one of these times: "I've never seen orange trees before. I remember sitting in the backyard behind the studio and just freaking out because of the orange trees!"

While working with Lavigne, The Matrix performed its magic in a studio known as Decoy Studios, which is found in the Los Angeles suburb of Valley Village. The team usually chooses to set up their studio in a rented house, as opposed to a conventionally commercial joint. They find that this relaxed setting creates a greater level of comfort for the artists they work with, which tends to get the creative juices flowing much more readily and also produces the best takes when recording. Moreover, all those involved in the process are more likely to feel at ease, without the tremendous costs that are involved in supporting a commercial property.

Scott Spock, who produced and engineered most of the tracks written at Decoy Studios, reinforces the benefit of these surroundings when he talks about his time spent with Avril.

"It works out great...because vocalists come in and they're very relaxed. They don't even realize that when they get on the mike, it's probably going to be on the record. With Avril, I think she thought she was cutting the demo of a song. The comfort level is very high working this way, and she's not standing in a $2500-a-day studio and thinking, 'Oh, my God, there's the engineer and this million-dollar board, and I've gotta sing this right 'cause it's going on the record!' She came in, she was really relaxed and she nailed it. 'Okay, Avril, that sounds good.' 'It does? Cool!'"

And so, the changes that went along with moving from east to west, including new cultural and visual stimulants, and understanding and knowledgeable songwriters in Clif Magness and The Matrix, rejuvenated a refreshed and reflective spark in her. These changes made all the difference to Avril Lavigne in the conceiving and recording of what would turn out to be her chart-busting debut album, *Let Go*.

reconnecting with nettwerk

Before the release of *Let Go*, however, there was one more change Avril had to make. After discussing it with her family, Avril decided that it was time to part company with manager Cliff Fabri. After her previously encouraging encounter with Nettwerk Records, Avril felt that the Vancouver-based company would be better able to fulfill her management needs. Accordingly, she contacted Nettwerk and arranged to meet with the CEO, Terry McBride. Judy Lavigne joined her daughter for the meeting at which they discussed the possibility of a management change, and together the three concluded that Nettwerk was the right fit for filling the role of Avril's management.

Terry would step in as Lavigne's manager and help guide her through the release of her debut album. Since the majority of the album had already been recorded, thanks to months of hard work by Avril, her collaborators and the many capable A&R staff members from Arista, Terry's role primarily involved creating a plan that best facilitated Avril's relationship with her label. Mark Jowett, who had from the beginning thought it best to support Avril's decision to sign with Arista, is certain that the freedom and encouragement Nettwerk had initially offered her was one reason for her return to them. "In a way, it was kind of like one of those karmic circles," he suggests lightheartedly.

Shauna Gold, one of Nettwerk's thriving young managers (now Senior Vice President of Artist Management), was a partner in Avril's management team along with Terry McBride right from the beginning. Gold, who started out as a receptionist at Nettwerk

12 years ago, is described by Jowett as "a beautiful person." And Avril, who obviously became very close to Gold, thanks her in the *Let Go* album insert, stating, "Shauna Gold…I love you woman!"

Priding themselves on their work with self-made artists such as Sarah McLachlan and the Barenaked Ladies, Nettwerk typically takes on musicians who can be classified as both singers and songwriters. As Terry McBride describes, "We only deal with real artists. I refused to get into the boy band/girl band dirge…in fact, I kept completely away from it. The principle of any artist we manage here is they write their own material, record their own material and perform their own material."

Avril obviously fit this mold, but what other values did she portray that encompassed the Nettwerk vision? Going along with the premise of a "self-made" musician, Avril exuded a kind of confidence in herself and her music that made her stand out from others who Nettwerk may have overlooked. Looking at the headstrong young Canadian girl who stood before them, the company knew that Avril was determined to tread her own path on her own terms.

Nettwerk continually encourages its artists to be themselves, to convey their personality and to connect with their audience through their music, and this belief was congruent with Lavigne's determination to do her own thing regardless of what others thought. As Mark Jowett explains, "I think what we try to do is not change people too much from where they are." He goes on to add that Nettwerk strives to make sure their artists "not [have]

AvRiL tRiViA
The punk band Good Charlotte parodied Avril
in their July 2003 video, "Girls and Boys."

their image and their music be divorced from their soul and their heart and who they are as people."

Today, an increasing portion of the music industry is built on unique superstars who have done just that. However, Avril's album was released at a time when pop music reigned and comprised a large number of, essentially, manufactured acts, such as Britney Spears and the Backstreet Boys, whose personas were likely constructed and modified according to existing trends. Arista also had a full roster of mainstream artists and may have felt pressured into modeling a rising teenage star such as Avril after a tried-and-true product like many of the current frontrunners on the Top 40 scene.

"I'm just coming out and I'm going to clearly be myself—I write what I feel, and I never worry what others think…I'm gonna dress what's me, I'm gonna act what's me and I'm gonna sing what's me," states Lavigne. Luckily, now that Avril had signed with the Nettwerk management group, McBride, Jowett and their capable staff shared and supported the young singer's words, helping her in maintaining her integrity and uniqueness as a performer.

In backing its artists' true originality, Nettwerk also tries to ensure that the musicians they work with, such as Avril, sustain themselves in an industry where so many people are thrown into the limelight quickly and fade away even faster. Although Avril may not always rise to the incredible heights of her current success, Mark Jowett certainly has faith in her talent and believes that she will have longevity in the music industry. He says that by "focusing more on her touring, her live base…her musicianship, and her songwriting…she will do very, very well…and really connect with people on a musical level for many years." One obvious thing about Lavigne is that she persistently tries to develop her own talent, which can only benefit her career in music as she continues to stay true to herself and evolve as a musician.

Besides believing in her compatibility with the principles of Nettwerk as an organization, Terry McBride also believed so strongly in Avril's talent that he was confident she was in good hands as far as her management was concerned. In a December 2002 interview with *Vancouver Magazine*, in which he was named one of Vancouver's 10 most powerful people, McBride went so far as to compare Avril to one of today's pioneering female artists, Sarah McLachlan, and predicted that Avril would change the way that people all over the world listened to music.

"Is Avril going to affect the next three to four years of music? Around the world? Oh yeah. Is she of the moment? A lot of her critics will say that, but Avril is no different than Sarah McLachlan 10 years ago. She's real. She writes her own stuff, she performs her own stuff, she won't let you change who and what she is. Sarah was the same stubborn, focused individual driven by the need just to be who and what she is. Those sorts of artists tend to last quite a long time. And they tend to drag a generation with them. Avril is going to drag a generation with her," McBride said.

Avril was also most likely comforted by the fact that Terry had a drive and a headstrong attitude similar to her own. Furthermore, he maintains a humility and resistance towards much of the hoopla that tends to surround the music industry. In the same interview in *Vancouver Magazine*, McBride demonstrated this humble outlook by saying, "Q magazine in England printed a list of the 50 most powerful people in the music business in the world and they ranked me at number 33. I find that hilarious. When it hits the shelves, I'll be ducking because, you know, I don't want this noise. I don't know how to react to this kind of thing. I just do what I do, you know?" In the liner notes of her album, Avril's admiration of Terry is obvious as she thanks him, saying, "You're my hero, it's an honor to work with you."

With McBride as her mentor and guide through the release of her debut album, as well as his and Jowett's infinite support for their young phenom's musical abilities and steadfast individuality, Avril was set up for success with a front-row view of the ups and downs and ins and outs of the music industry. And with access to Nettwerk's resources, an organization that currently manages at least eight artists who sell millions of albums, Avril was in good company.

With a loving family at home, a highly thriving label on her side and the insight of Nettwerk's management team in her back pocket, Avril definitely had a solid support. Finally, after several years of toiling away in her bedroom in Napanee, on stage at country fairs and then in studios across the United States with the industry's top songwriters, Avril Lavigne was ready to move full speed ahead with the release of her debut album, *Let Go*.

time to let go

At last, all was in place, and Avril Lavigne was ready to be introduced to the world. Her debut album, *Let Go*, was released on June 4, 2002, to an unsuspecting audience. Her listeners, of course, were knee-deep in the boy-band era in which groups such as 'N Sync, the Backstreet Boys and 98 Degrees ruled the international stage. They were used to seeing teenage girls, such as Britney Spears, Christina Aguilera and Mandy Moore, dressed in tight clothing and flawlessly executing choreographed dance numbers with a slew of professional backup dancers who had many more years of performing behind them than their leader. The radios were filled with songs about fairytale love, which most of the young singers had yet to experience.

And then came Avril Lavigne. Having never experienced anything like this girl before, the world did not know what to expect. All of a sudden, this 5-foot-nothing firecracker was shouting out lyrics about being real, staying true to yourself and doing what you want. While her delicate features and pretty hair said one thing, her studded bracelets, baggy pants, Doc Martens and the "I stole it from my dad's closet" tie around her neck screamed something completely different. She had attitude, she had style, and she had a voice that could be heard from one end of a football field to the other.

Youth everywhere were in a frenzy, requesting her music on the radio and her videos on TV, and raiding their fathers' wardrobes for a cool tie to wear to school. At the time, many assumed that Avril Lavigne was a product of her record company. No one knew that she was a self-made, small-town girl from Napanee, Ontario, who got her start in her church choir and at country fairs. And at first, no one seemed to care either, as they rushed out to buy the hottest album on the block. Within four months of its release,

Let Go sold over two million copies in Canada, earning Lavigne double-platinum status in her home country.

Her first single, "Complicated," broke records on the Canadian Contemporary Hit Radio Charts, remaining on top for 11 unprecedented weeks. This was a major accomplishment, taking the record away from none other than the legendary Madonna, who had held the top spot for her 2000 hit "Music." In less than six months, the Recording Industry Association of America (RIAA) certified the album four times platinum.

> Communicating closely with her fans from the onset of her public success, Lavigne wrote a journal entry on her website soon after the release of *Let Go*. In true teenage excitement she wrote, "So my CD is out now!!! It came out on the fourth. It was a special day for me. In a way it felt like my birthday. I'd like to thank everyone who purchased a copy. Your support is much appreciated!"

And that was only the beginning for Lavigne. *Let Go* went on to be an international success and has now sold over 15 million copies worldwide. The album earned number one spots on charts in Canada, the United Kingdom and Australia, and peaked at number two in the United States. With a successful collection of four singles coming from the album, Avril became the superstar she had always dreamed of being. Nevertheless, the 17-year-old remained surprisingly levelheaded concerning her album's success on the charts, saying, "I didn't ever think about the charts, because I never knew about them until I got into the business. But I did always believe in myself."

AvRiL tRiViA

At the dawning of this new era in music, powerful female performers began to emerge that put the Spice Girls to shame. Disregarding the industry-pressured fabrication of princesses past, these young female pioneers had self-made talent, songwriting skills, drive and personality, all of which were being carefully nurtured by a visionary set of A&R reps and record company executives.

It was apparent to them that artists such as Michelle Branch, Vanessa Carlton and Avril Lavigne were the wave of the future, as their audiences were rapidly becoming more knowledgeable and sophisticated about the music they listened to. Spectators were easily impressed by these beautiful young girls who wrote their own material, played their own instruments and broke new ground in the mainstream music world.

Avril Lavigne's *Let Go* reaped the benefits of this rising age of solo superstars because, unlike her counterparts, she experienced a great deal of success in the overseas markets. Her debut album was also honored for being the highest-selling album in North America during 2002. And though the album received mixed reviews from the press, its sales made it obvious that Avril had made many more fans than enemies.

let go:
the album

What made people turn their heads when they heard Lavigne's music was the unique sound that she brought to the table. Obviously pop-influenced, with its catchy melodies and global appeal to teeny boppers, her sound also maintained an edginess that made quite an impression on the average listener. Punk-like guitar riffs and crazy rock 'n' roll drumming gave the music a sharpness that separated it from artists such as Vanessa Carlton and her mellow piano accompaniment. Additionally, Avril's powerful voice was captivating, wailing in Alanis Morissette-like fashion over the band's serious state of loudness. This combination of pop, punk, rock and alternative, in addition to the unwaveringly wild persona of Avril and her bandmates, was enough to blow away audiences of all ages.

Avril's original sound can be heard right from the surprising opening song on the album, "Losing Grip." The track, written during her sessions with Clif Magness, is the fourth single from *Let Go* and is also Avril's favorite song on the album. Perhaps the most powerful song from the *Let Go* collection, "Losing Grip" shows the amazing dynamic range of Avril's voice. Displaying a more delicate side during its reflective verses, the song is about a misleading romance in which a girl's so-called partner seems more caught up in his own life than in caring for her.

The chorus blows up into musical and emotional dissonance as Avril tunefully screams at full force that she refuses to be treated that way. Reminiscent of fellow Canadian Alanis Morissette's "bitter lover" syndrome on her *Jagged Little Pill* album, "Losing Grip" is a look into where the album could have gone had Avril continued working along her initial path with Magness.

Although this style may have brought her a slew of new fans, it is probably a good thing that she didn't follow that path because the song only peaked at number 64 on the Billboard Hot 100 in the U.S. "Losing Grip" still managed to do well at home, however, reaching number one in Canada, and it did fairly well in the United Kingdom, Europe and Taiwan. Lavigne explains that her inspiration for the song came from a relationship with a guy she once dated. "I was this guy's girlfriend, and he didn't even treat me like it…If he sat there with his arm around me, it was just because I was his chick." Sounds as if he deserved this song!

Next on the album is the song that took everyone by storm and is now known as Avril's signature song—"Complicated." Written during that fateful first writing session with The Matrix, the song is remembered by Lauren Christy for the impact it had on some of her industry friends before the release of the album. "Somebody in the industry sat us down and said, 'I'd bet my house that this song is going to go to number one,'" Christy says.

That person was absolutely right—the song burst to number one on the Canadian Singles Chart. Her country also paid tribute to Avril with several honors for "Complicated," awarding her gold and platinum single certifications from the Canadian Recording Industry Association for selling over 100,000 copies of her single. Additionally, the track won her the 2003 Juno Award for Single of the Year, one of the most prestigious awards in the Canadian recording industry.

Catching hold of the top spot on several Billboard charts for many weeks, Avril was recognized in the United States for her success with "Complicated," securing two Grammy nominations for Best Female Pop Vocal Performance and Song of the Year. Unfortunately, both awards went to fellow female singing sensation, Norah Jones. Lavigne also nabbed number one spots in Australia, Mexico and on the Radio Express World Chart Show. "Complicated" picked up an MTV Award and several awards at the Radio Disney Awards, including Best Song, and it even came away with the title of Best Homework Song!

One of the most popular songs of 2002, "Complicated" ruled the radio airwaves across North America and broke an unbelievable record. Fellow Canadians and rock stars in their own right, Nickelback had set a record in 2001 for most plays on American radio in a single week with an incredible 9050 spins, which averages about one play per minute, 24 hours a day, seven days a week! Avril and her team could not believe their ears when they heard that she had broken that record with a mind-boggling 9205 spins in only one week!

The song itself is the most radio-ready track on *Let Go*, with a memorable chorus and a strong message to be yourself. It talks about Avril's wish that the guy she is dating would stop trying to be someone he's not, proclaiming that she likes him better when he's not trying so hard—quite a statement coming from a 17-year-old.

Although "Complicated" is extremely pop-influenced, it still maintains the edginess in its lyrics and in Avril's voice that turned heads at its release. Rumor has it that the singer did not even like the song that much and considered leaving it off *Let Go*, but an A&R rep insisted that she put it on the record. Maybe she's now glad she did.

"Sk8r Boi," with its unique spelling, is the second single from the album and was a smash hit. The song tells the story of a young romance between a skater boy and a prissy ballerina. She decides to ditch the guy because of what her friends say, or as Avril puts it, "he wasn't good enough for her." Co-written by The Matrix, the song ends with the ballerina, who is now a single mother, watching the skater boy, now a famous rock star, punk out on stage and fall in love with Avril instead. This charming tale, combined with its upbeat tempo, wicked guitar riffs and endless energy, made "Sk8r Boi" a popular anthem for youth everywhere and once again carried a powerful underlying message about peer pressure and acceptance.

After the release of the single, fans grew even closer to Avril as they witnessed different sides of her in the song, which shows her as a hardcore skater girl, a pop-rocker with attitude and a hopeless romantic all in one. Topping the Canadian charts, the track also made the top 10 on multiple Billboard charts in the United States (including a number one on the Top 40 Mainstream chart), as well as on charts in many countries around the globe.

AvRiL tRiViA
During the filming of the video for "Sk8r Boi,"
the director of the video gave Avril $100 for
keeping a dead cockroach on her tongue for
10 seconds.

Because of the extensive narration in "Sk8r Boi," most people believed that it was a story too complex to have been made up, and they assumed it was about Avril. Frustrated by the question, she is quick to clarify. "So many people ask me that...No, it's not...[It's drawn from] what I went through in high school and what I saw in high school, and how different people acted and treated each other." Finally the truth comes out. "I just kind of took that and put it into a story. I wasn't talking about a certain guy or girl."

"Sk8r Boi" did very well by the critics and picked up its share of awards, starting with a Nickelodeon's Kid Choice Award for Best Song, which demonstrated her obvious appeal to a younger audience. In June 2003 the song also brought home two Much Music Awards, one for Best International Video by a Canadian and another for Best Canadian Artist. And although she wasn't awarded any Grammys, she was recognized for her edgy quality with a nomination for Best Rock Vocal Performance. One critic from the United Kingdom even went so far as to say, "'Sk8er Boi' is brilliant. It's a classic high-energy pop song with crunchy guitars and a great hook...It bowls you over with its energy and sticks in your mind. It's one of the best tracks on this...debut album."

Avril slows things down with her next song on the album, "I'm With You," a beautiful ballad that was the third successful single from *Let Go*. The track opens with a sensual cello line played by Suzi Katayama, a regular in the recording industry who has played, conducted or arranged tracks on hit albums for artists such as Prince, Duran Duran, Faith Hill, k.d. lang and Alanis Morissette. "I'm With You" was not released in Australia, but it qualified as Lavigne's third number one single in Canada and allowed her to once again top several Billboard charts.

By far the most emotional track on the album, the song entrances its listeners and explores a young girl's loneliness, reflection and teenage angst. Although the instrumentation is rather simplistic, the arrangement uses an excellent dynamic range to enforce the power and passion behind Lavigne's voice.

Avril had a strong connection with the single during its recording, saying, "I went into the booth to sing it with just so much emotion. I had, like, goosebumps going down my spine. It was really neat." She was mesmerized by the song, adding, "When I sing that song, I just like to stand there in my own world. That is an important song for me." It was an important track for The Matrix too, as they had just scored their third number one hit of the album with "I'm With You," which boosted them into songwriting superstardom in the music community. The single was certified platinum and helped to establish Lavigne's strength as a vocal performer.

The fifth track on the album, "Mobile," could have been the fifth single with its easy but likable chorus and head-bopping beat. It was actually released as a single down under, reaching number 26 on the charts in New Zealand, but the rest of the world had to buy the album to hear the track. Documenting Avril's ever-changing life since becoming a professional singer, the lyrics from "Mobile" talk about the sacrifices she made and the lack of control she has over her life.

Despite its rather depressing topic, the song maintains an upbeat nature, backed up by spunky acoustic and electric guitars, and also includes an interlude of la la las for the audience to happily join in on. A product of Avril's sessions with Clif Magness, the song somewhat preserves an edgier sound with the slightly more abrasive guitar strumming in the chorus, but it is generally pretty tame compared to the tracks "Unwanted" and "Losing Grip."

Overall, "Mobile" is definitely a pop song, from its basic form (verse-chorus-verse-chorus-bridge-chorus-chorus-chorus) down to the chorus breakdown (the part where everything calms down and she quietly sings the chorus) right before the la la las that lead into the final chorus. Most likely a crowd favorite at concerts, the track is a tunefully charming addition to *Let Go*.

Arguably the most angry song on the album, "Unwanted" opens with the loud, harsh, swinging guitars reminiscent of a Nirvana song. In 3 minutes and 41 seconds, this track sums up the anger Avril felt towards the parents of a past boyfriend who had made a judgment about her prior to meeting her. True to her religious family's values, Avril appreciates the importance of getting to know the family of your significant other and treating them with respect.

However, the respect was not returned in this case. "I was really polite to them. I had dinner with them at the table, and I had my manners, like, 'Can I help you with anything? Can I wash the dishes?' But they didn't want me with their boy. I guess they thought I was a bit wild for him. And I was so hurt by that." Lucky for her, she came out on top with a smashing track on her multiplatinum album. We can only wonder how those parents now feel about the way they treated her.

"Unwanted" was the first successful collaboration that resulted from Avril's venture out West and was written in her first writing session with Clif Magness. After hearing the song, coupled with the album's other, rather enraged, track, "Losing Grip," record executives were taken aback by the sound that the former country-singing Canadian had produced. Even L.A. Reid stated, "I was actually quite surprised to see the direction things took, because I thought it would be a little more…folky." But as Avril continued to work with Magness, and of course The Matrix writing team, "Unwanted" and "Losing Grip" became only a piece of the multi-dimensional puzzle that made up *Let Go.*

Joining "I'm With You" in the softer ballad category, "Tomorrow" is a melancholy tune about the uncertain future of a (most likely) romantic relationship. The simple and unassuming composition expresses the ambiguity of Avril's thoughts regarding a situation between herself and this other mystery person. It is a rather mature topic for a girl of only 17 to undertake, and she responsibly decides to wait it out to see where her feelings are "Tomorrow." One of the few works that was not a product of her partnerships with either Magness or The Matrix, this largely acoustic track is a nice break from the electric sounds of many of the other heavier songs on *Let Go.*

"Tomorrow" was co-written with Avril by Curtis Frasca and Sabelle Breer, who are currently a thriving songwriting duo in the music industry. Having worked with such revered artists as Céline Dion, Frasca and Breer are presently most renowned for their affiliation with pop prince Ryan Cabrera. Although not quite a smash hit, "Tomorrow" is a calming combination of sweet simplicity and reflective emotion that pleasantly reveals a softer side of Avril Lavigne.

"Anything But Ordinary" is the perfect way to describe Avril and the life she now leads. The song was originally used as the title on the press kit that was sent out regarding her debut album release, and a record executive once suggested to Avril that it be used as the title of her album as well. The longest track on the album, which ended up with the title *Let Go* instead (which, incidentally, was named after a track that was not included on the album), describes how antsy Lavigne might have felt if she had the lifestyle of an average person. Preferring to catch a plane to London for a press conference, do a photo shoot for *YM Magazine*, answer questions in an interview at Much Music or rock out on stage in Tokyo, the young superstar claims, "This is my lifestyle, but I wouldn't want a normal life or I'd get bored."

"Anything But Ordinary" starts out with the typically teenage lyrics, "Sometimes I get so weird, I even freak myself out," but later offers more complex subject matter by contemplating the meaning and validity of her existence, which is another unexpectedly complicated topic for a teenager to assume. Avril is always pushing the boundaries and doing her best to stand out in a crowd, so it is easy to see— especially for The Matrix, who co-wrote the song with her— that this girl has always been destined for the extraordinary.

The most admirable quality of songwriters is the ability to extract the thoughts, feelings and experiences from their life and verbalize them in a way that relates to others. Even though most people think that they are alone in what they are going through, songs such as "Things I'll Never Say," the ninth track of *Let Go*, help them realize that this is not the case. Describing what probably happens to most girls who fall for a guy, whether a teenager or not, the song talks about being nervous around this certain someone and the inability to be themselves—by "stutter"-ing and "stumble"-ing through a conversation with them.

In the song, Avril also sings about the age-old fantasy of a guy proposing to a girl "on one knee." Another track by The Matrix, "Things I'll Never Say" opens with folky and rhythmic la la las and revisits the acoustic guitars of earlier songs on the album, accompanied by a refreshing melody and an easy-to-relate-to theme.

While there was not much going on in Napanee to keep Avril busy when she was growing up, she still holds the town close to her heart. She talks about her hometown in the next song on the album, "My World." Another deviation from the original roughness resulting from her collaboration with Clif Magness, this extremely "poppy" song talks about her childhood "in a five thousand population town" where she "never wore cover-up, always beat the boys up," and "made…money by cutting grass."

One of the most melodic tracks on *Let Go*, the song's bubblegum backbeat and lofty topic of daydreaming about a future love are occasionally offset by the lyrics of a pop rebel, with lines like "Got fired by fried chicken a**" and "Though it might take a friggin' day." Another strong and well-constructed addition to the album, "My World" was later taken on as the name of her first DVD release of one of her live shows. With a look into her suburban upbringing and some of her everyday thoughts, Avril reels in her fans with this lighthearted, yet meaningful, contribution to *Let Go*.

Despite the fact that Avril was not happy with some of her early efforts in writing with more-experienced songwriters and rejected many of the original songs for the album, one of the songs she kept was "Nobody's Fool," written with Peter Zizzo. The song may not be the strongest track on *Let Go*, but it certainly has unique qualities that separate it from others on the album. For example, the verses are rapped instead of sung. And though rapping may not be one of her most highly acclaimed skills, Lavigne at least possesses the right, strong-willed attitude for the song, which still contains yet another catchy, sing-along chorus.

With a more laid-back feeling than other songs on the album, "Nobody's Fool" highlights the idea of being yourself and sends the straightforward message that if you don't like what you see, tough, because I ain't changin' for no one! Zizzo, who also produced the track in his New York studio, joined Avril on the guitars on the *Let Go* recording as well. Perhaps a personal anthem to the record executives and to the rest of the world, "Nobody's Fool" is a welcome addition to the album and an ode to Avril's continuous determination to set her own path.

Clif Magness' final contribution to the album is "Too Much To Ask," which follows the edgier characteristics of the previous Magness/Lavigne tracks and uses harsher, more abrasive guitars and more of a rock vibe. The song, however, is not quite as gripping as "Losing Grip" or "Unwanted," perhaps because its message is not as easy to relate to, but also because the writers did not take as many risks melodically and lyrically. With the musical arrangement being rather predictable, and the lyrics rather simple, the tune does not do much to be memorable.

One thing for which you can give Lavigne credit is for once again using a negative experience from her own life and turning it into a song on a brilliantly successful album. In "Too Much To Ask," she sings about a summer crush who blew her off many times in favor of smoking pot. Summed up in the line: "It's funny when you think it's gonna work out 'til you chose weed over me, you're so lame," Avril explains what happened that summer, "He'd choose to go get high instead of be with me in certain situations. He was never my boyfriend or anything. I was pissed off at the summer crush. I mean, he was a dick. I liked him. And I wanted something. And he liked me. But if I had a boyfriend, I would cherish him so much."

She then goes on to reveal her rarely seen softer side, saying, "I might look like a tough chick—and I am—but I'm also a hopeless romantic inside." While not the biggest hit of the album, "Too Much To Ask" does just fine in clarifying the pop-rocker's antidrug stance, a subject often associated with heavy guitars and rock music, and one from which she wishes to dissociate herself.

The final track on *Let Go*, "Naked" portrays none of the rebellion or the stand-out-in-a-crowd outlook of other tracks on the album but, instead, displays a side of Avril that is gentle and vulnerable, a quality the media so often overlooks. The young songwriter again worked with veterans Curtis Frasca and Sabelle Breer on what is the only positively influenced love song on the album. An introspective and mature way of concluding her debut album, the song describes how someone can feel so exposed in love, and the mixed feelings of fear, happiness and excitement that often accompany a new relationship.

These opposing emotions are well represented in the different harmonic progressions throughout the song, and Avril surprises listeners once again with her extremely grown-up lyrics, which sound as though they were written by someone twice her age. The chorus of "Naked" demonstrates what is probably the most country influence of the album, with the combination of some slightly more twanging guitars and Avril's signature chorusing effect (where she sings with herself, sounding like a chorus of Avrils). Overall, "Naked" is a beautiful conclusion to a widely diverse album, simply adding to the complexity of *Let Go*'s multi-dimensional success.

let go makes an impact

Thirteen tracks later, with over 15 million albums sold, *Let Go* went beyond the achievements ever imagined by Arista Records, Nettwerk and Avril and her family. Avril Lavigne's debut album surpassed the designation of "smash hit," and she now had millions of fans all over the world. Ecstatic with the results of her first attempt as a professional recording artist, Avril was also pleased with the way that *Let Go* represented the variety in her personality. "It really shows all the different sides of me. I'm a person with a ton of energy who likes to scream and party and rock out, and there are other sides of me that are real serious."

The album covers issues that a middle-aged person might find difficult to put into words, but Avril explained where she developed the mature point of view that is so evident throughout the album. "I've been through a lot because I'm in the [music] business and it's aged me," she explains. "I've had to take care of myself and make really important decisions, and I'm around adults 24-7."

Proud of her debut album, Avril was also excited to be nominated for a Grammy (or five!) at only 17 years of age and to be able to share the thrilling experience with her family. "It's just the coolest thing to go home and be like, 'Mom and Dad, I got nominated for a Grammy,'" she marveled during an interview with CBS's *Early Morning*.

Although she did not win any awards out of her Grammy nominations, Avril had the amazing opportunity to perform at the awards show. With a viewing audience of over two billion people,

Avril blew the crowd away by performing "Sk8r Boi" with the same outstanding vivacity that got her the nominations.

Just as "Complicated" had set records in its weekly number of spins, *Let Go* also achieved an industry best in America as the first album by a solo artist to see rising sales for five consecutive weeks. Additionally, the album picked up a slew of awards domestically, winning Avril an impressive four Juno awards in 2003 (out of six nominations), including Pop Album of the Year, New Artist of the Year and Album of the Year.

Suitably, the Juno Awards ceremony was held in Ottawa at the Corel Centre, and Avril collected her awards on the same stage that, at the age of 14, she once shared with Shania Twain. It was also where she had proclaimed to Shania that she would one day be a famous singer.

Furthermore, Lavigne was honored at the 2003 Canadian Radio Music Awards with another set of four awards: Best New Group or Solo Artist, Fans' Choice Award, the SOCAN (Society of Composers, Authors and Music Publishers of Canada) Songwriter of the Year Award and Best New Solo Artist (Rock).

Avril also was acknowledged in the United States at the Radio Disney Awards and even went back to New York City to accept the 2002 MTV Video Music Award for Best New Artist. Moreover, she brought home the ASCAP (American Society of Composers, Authors and Publishers) award for Most Performed Song in a Motion Picture, for the song "I'm With You" from the movie *Bruce Almighty* (2003).

AvRiL tRiViA
Avril was once given a rabbit as a gift
from a fan in Korea.

In addition, Avril made appearances on several talk shows to showcase her debut album, including *Regis & Kelly*, *The Late Late Show with Craig Kilborn* and *The Tonight Show with Jay Leno*, appealing to listeners all over the clock. One of her songs was even featured in the coveted 2002 season finale episode of *Felicity*, an extremely popular *O.C.*-type college drama loved by millions of viewers.

Let Go had sold so many albums by the end of 2002 that its sales were only topped by the albums *Nellyville* and *The Eminem Show*. Avril revealed to *Chart* magazine that even the controversial rapper dug her music, saying, "Eminem told me he respected my album, shook my hand and walked away." She goes on to share another tale of celebrity acclamation, saying, "I walked into P. Diddy's party, and he gets up on the mike and yells, 'Avril Lavigne's in the house.'" It seems North America had Avril Lavigne fever!

Lavigne's efforts with her debut album were also recognized internationally. At the larger-than-life Brit Awards in 2003, Avril was nominated for two awards, namely, International

AvRiL tRiViA

Prince Harry invited Avril to play at his annual
charity concert in Hyde Park and admitted to
a journalist that he thought she was pretty.

Breakthrough Artist, which saw a repeat of the Grammys with
Norah Jones winning, and International Female Solo Artist,
which went to fellow Arista recording artist, Pink. Avril, however,
made a special trip to Singapore to sing for 8000 pumped fans at
the 2003 MTV Asia Awards, where she won several awards, for
Favorite Breakthrough Artist, Favorite Female Artist and the Style
Award as well. Avril Lavigne had become a genuine international
superstar!

And so, after taking the world by storm with her debut album,
Let Go, and gaining much acclaim from both insiders and out-
siders in the industry, Avril Lavigne proved that she was a force to
be reckoned with. The young Canadian singing sensation was on
an upward-moving mission and was ready to do whatever it took
to establish herself as a long-term resident in record stores
around the globe.

the closet of a sk8er girl

For decades the general public has looked to celebrities, such as actors, singers and athletes, for the latest fashion dos and don'ts. If we saw a friend walking down the street wearing furry boots outside of their jeans, we might do a double take and ask her what she did to her dog and why she was wearing it on her feet. However, when Mischa Barton or Lindsay Lohan stroll down the sidewalks of Hollywood wearing an original pair of Australian Ugg boots, complete with Miss Sixty slim-fit jeans lazily tucked into them, we cannot run fast enough to the nearest luxury shoe store to pay an exorbitant amount of money for our own pair.

In our current society of uncontrollable consumerism, it is rather unnerving that teenage celebrities (and celebrities in general) are considered products to be marketed in as many different facets as possible, including in the world of fashion. As a result, not only do young stars have to manufacture their talent in order to be successful, but they must also maintain the right "look." The look is usually flawless, brand-driven, constantly changing and continuously under the scrutiny of the public and the press. Sounds like a lot of pressure!

But for Avril Lavigne, the pressure to dress a certain way first came up in high school, long before she became the fashion diva she is today. "There was a group of girls who sat at the same table in the cafeteria every day. They all wore Gap T-shirts and Abercrombie and Fitch," she recalls. "I remember trying to be friends with them because they were so popular. But they were so cliquish."

Instead, Avril hung out with the skater boys, which is where she developed the personal style that made an incredible impact upon the release of her debut album. "I wrote my first album when I was a 16-year-old skater who wore size 32 pants and hoodies," she says of her pre-celebrity look. "I was a tomboy. I had an older brother I looked up to, and I hung out with mostly guys."

When Cliff Fabri first started working with Avril, he was well aware that her sense of style, much like her choice of music at the time, was limited and a little bit all over the place. He was patient, however, and allowed her to mature at her own speed, which for Avril, was usually at warp speed. By the time *Let Go* was ready to hit the record stores, Avril Lavigne merchandise hit the clothing racks as well. From the fashionably ambiguous childhood she was leading before her blast into stardom, the Canadian teenager had transformed herself into a distinctively styled sensation who changed the way kids dressed around the globe.

Picture this: baggy pants shuffling down her hips and ending three quarters of the way down her legs, plain tank tops or T-shirts fronted with skulls or various obscenities, studded leather wristbands, big belt buckles, simple sneakers or combat boots and a tie that looked like it came from her dad's closet. Her attire was not quite the diamond-studded bustiers, hip-hugging jeans and revealing belly tops that many of the bubblegum princesses who topped the charts at the time sported!

It honestly sounds more like something you could purchase at the local thrift store, but that was probably the idea. Although it was difficult (and most of the time inappropriate) for 13-year-old girls to wear the short, shimmery shirts and tight, teasing bottoms of most female pop stars, the clothes Avril wore were readily available in local shopping centers, in skate shops, and even in the closets of these girls' fathers and brothers. Mothers may not have been pleased about the quantity of black their young girls wore, and perhaps the lack of femininity they assumed, but they could not really complain about the amount of skin shown and the loose-fitting garments their daughters now donned.

Although not completely conventional, this style of dress was accessible to youth—they could buy its components at the mall, it was within their budget and was, of course, accompanied by a bit of a rebellious mind-set that usually appeals to teenagers. As L.A. Reid remarks, "Kids feel they can identify with Avril. They wear the same T-shirt, the same jeans, have the same kind of nonchalant attitude."

Many critics swore that Avril's record company forced this antipop-princess image on Avril, but she quickly claimed otherwise, saying, "Nobody tells me what to wear. Trust me." Even songwriter Peter Zizzo is unwavering in his stance regarding the young girl's appearance, stating, "...what you see imagewise is who she was from day one in terms of the fatigues and the tank tops. There's a lot of people out there who think this is somehow a look that was put together for her, but nothing could be further from the truth."

So what exactly does Avril Lavigne wear? Let's go from top to bottom, starting with the trademark tie that she sports around her neck. Avril first championed her signature tie in the video for her debut single, "Complicated," in which she wore a plain black tie, as well as a more festive red plaid one. This is probably the single most distinguishing element of her early look, spawning an international trend that turned ties from dudwear to studwear in 10 seconds or less. After complaining for years about the tie some of them had to wear with their school uniform, teenage girls now stole ties from their unsuspecting fathers and tied them loosely around their necks on weekends, which surely must have confused their parents.

Avril, who at first implied that she was fairly "anti-fashion," was initially excited by the idea that she had started a trend. In her online journal in June 2002, she wrote, "I noticed at every show we've had, some of the girls have been wearing tank tops and ties like me... :) ...so I now have 'Avril' ties in my merchandise." She wore ties for just over a year, until she one day looked out into the crowd and realized that there was a sea full of Avril clones in the audience. She decided it was time to put the tie to rest.

What did she do with all of her ties? She fills the fans in: "I wore one every day for a year, maybe longer, and then I gave all the ties away that I didn't want and kept the ones I did want." She goes on to say, "I have a treasure trunk at home, and I keep them there. I still have my tie that I wore for the videos, still knotted with the same knot, and I still have my Grammy tie. I'm very sentimental."

Also around her neck during the tie era were a slew of necklaces with various charms, among them a black star, a gold V-shaped electric guitar, a silver skull, a massive cross and another gold one with classy cursive writing that seemed to involve some sort of expletive (in pure rock star fashion, of course).

> In the first couple of years of her career, Avril was usually seen in loose-fitting baby tees, generally in dark colors (black, gray, brown or navy), but she sometimes wore more vibrant colors, such as the vintage-style, bright green T-shirt with yellow writing that she wore in her "Sk8er Boi" video.

Apparently, one particular T-shirt that Avril wore during her appearance on *Saturday Night Live* caused quite a stir in her hometown of Napanee. On January 11, 2003, she appeared on the show sporting an orange-colored Home Hardware Napanee shirt, which evidently was her soccer jersey when she was five. Dustin Bee, the manager of the store at the time, could not believe his eyes when he sat down to watch the show that night. He suddenly realized what the shirt said. "I couldn't believe it at first, took a second look, realized it was Home Hardware, saw the Napanee underneath," remembers Dustin.

Within minutes of the show, the answering machine at the hardware store was full. The phone continued to ring off the hook the following day, all calls from Avril Lavigne fans from all over North America who wanted to know where they could get their very own Home Hardware Napanee T-shirt. Although Dustin and his father, Dale, who owns the store, could never have afforded the $1,125,000 it would have cost for that kind of advertising, they did reap the rewards of the impromptu publicity, including hundreds of T-shirt orders following the *Saturday Night Live* episode. But it was not the store that benefited financially from the T-shirt sales. The proceeds from the sales went to a soccer team from the Greater Napanee Soccer Association, which the store had sponsored in previous years for only $175. The team got much more than that!

Avril, who was excited to hear that her clothing choice had made such an impact, expressed her wish that all of the T-shirts be manufactured in Napanee in order to benefit her hometown. This re-issue of the Home Hardware Napanee T-shirts must have helped the town out a great deal as the store sold somewhere in the neighborhood of 2000 shirts. It's amazing what eight minutes of advertising can do for a business!

Avril was also famous for wearing "wife-beater" tank tops. She wore them all the time, with a tie of choice, to public appearances, in videos (she wore two tank tops in the "Complicated" video), as well as wearing them on her own time. She is a big fan of the classic tank, and it is probably the most revealing piece of clothing on her body (but stay tuned for a baggy-pant story that may prove otherwise!).

> Wearing T-shirts and tank tops certainly doesn't do much to keep a person warm, so what does Avril do to remedy that? One approach, which she used in her "Complicated" video, is to wear something that can only be described as an "arm warmer." In the video, she wears a black and white striped arm sock on one arm, which is supposedly more of a fashion statement than an attempt to keep warm.

In her "I'm With You" video, she is much more successful at keeping warm, donning an oversized black parka while morosely wandering the streets on a cold, wet night. Okay, so maybe staying

AvRiL tRiViA

The shirt that Avril wore on the cover of *YM*
with Usher was actually a designer dress that
she didn't want to wear, so she cut it up.

warm wasn't Avril's main objective, but her arms do make an interesting fashion study.

In her early days, Avril was known for her plethora of black bracelets, everything from thin plastic ones wrapped multiple times around her wrists to black leather ones with dog collar–like metal studs, to other funky leather bands—always in black of course, in order to maintain her skater girl air. In one live performance, she even wrapped a one-inch-wide black leather strip all the way up both arms. She was also famous for wearing wristbands (similar to the kind that athletes wear), sometimes in black (such as in the "I'm With You" video) and sometimes in many colors (like the red, blue, and white one she wore on her right wrist during her *Saturday Night Live* performance).

Among other accessories that have made Avril a trendsetter are the big-buckled belts she sometimes wears to keep her baggy pants from falling down around her ankles, such as the one she wore during an appearance on the BBC show *Top of the Pop*, which was big and silver and said "COWLIFE" on it (still not sure what that means). Other belts she has worn include a thick white one with red stars all the way around it and a large, rectangle buckle with a symbol and the words "CAUTION BIOHAZARD" on it, as well as a black belt with a massive silver skull and crossbones for a buckle. Avril has one belt in particular that has turned a few heads. The belt buckle boldly states (in no less than capital letters) "F***." On a brief video clip on the MTV website, Avril attempts to hide some of the letters on the buckle, as the *David Letterman Show* told her that it was too offensive to be worn in its original form on the air. "Should I cover the 'F' or the 'CK,'" she wonders, and playfully decides to cover the 'CK' so that 'FU' will remain.

Otherwise, Avril has also worn metal-studded belts, as well as some more classic black and brown leather ones and, seen more often in her early look, standard linen belts that matched either her pants or T-shirt. Additionally, she wears wallet chains that hang down the side of her pants and are usually attached to the belt loops: a typical look for a skater girl.

When she was first introduced to the world in 2002, Avril tended to stay true to her tomboy childhood, from the waist down. Her underwear elastic crept over the top of her loose-fitting pants, which rested comfortably below her hips. For Avril, it's a toss-up between full-length and three-quarter-length pants, and her favorite brand of pantwear is Dickies, which has been making "quality workwear since 1922."

According to the Dickies website, Avril revealed to *Cosmopolitan* magazine that she "prefers Dickies to designer duds." It's no wonder that she likes them, as the workwear brand is a fave of a long line of celebrities in the music industry, including Lisa Marie Presley, the band My Chemical Romance, Fergie from the Black Eyed Peas and John Mayer. These pants must be comfy!

Avril and her fellow singing pals were also known to wear other Dickies duds, such as coveralls, shirts and tanks. Sporting a pair of the infamous pants at the 2002 Much Music Video Awards, Avril's Dickies were a little on the low side, revealing more of her than was really called for. Britney and Christina can parade around wearing a bra and panties on stage, but Avril's uninvited butt crack made international news! Was the young starlet embarrassed? Not at all! In fact, after letting the press know that this was not an intentional act of rebellion, she laughed off the event, arriving at the 2003 awards with the initials M-M-V-A written on her bum! According to the Much Music website, Avril mooned the press, posed for international photographers and ended up in newspapers and magazines all over North America, the United Kingdom, Asia, Norway, Argentina and Australia!

Although pants were Lavigne's usual attire a few years back, she occasionally showed her feminine side by wearing a skirt, such as the black-and-plaid number that she modeled on the cover of the March 2003 issue of *Rolling Stone*. Other than that, the most feminine clothing you were likely to see Avril wearing back then was something along the lines of the black pants with pink pinstripes along with a black satin bustier top held together with safety pins that she wore to the 2003 MTV Video Music Awards. Of course the "*Rolling Stone* skirt" was offset by thigh-high, black-and-red striped socks and combat boots. Besides colorful socks, she'll also go for a pair of knee-high, horizontally striped tube sport socks any day.

Covering her choice of socks most of the time are one of two things. "I need a walk-in closet. I have 20 million pairs of Converse and Doc Martens boots," she tells a fan. The "1460," a classic style of Doc Martens, is a common boot in rock history. Following in the footsteps of bands such as The Who and the Foo Fighters, Avril apparently once arrived at an interview for *Newsweek* in her less-than-dainty steel-toed Docs, complemented by a jacket with a pin on it that said, "F*** FASHION." That is quite the comment from the little girl who was unknowingly altering the fashion trends across the board!

When the Dr. Martens company offered to make Avril a customized pair of boots, she jumped at the chance. They then asked her what she wanted to have written on the tag on the back of the boots and, maintaining her rebellious streak, she told them that she wanted the word "F***" put on them! Would you believe she also chose the word "B****" when they offered to make her a second pair?!

She also loves her Converse sneakers. Originally invented by Chuck Taylor in 1917, this classic sneaker was initially made for basketball players but worked its way into rock history largely because of Kurt Cobain of Nirvana, who was constantly seen wearing them in photographs (he was even found wearing a pair after his tragic suicide). Converse is now a staple of many in the artsy community, and Avril gladly continues the legacy with her own classic black pair (or maybe a few pairs) of ankle highs that retail for about $40, far from designer costs.

> As far as the rocker piercings and tattoos go, Avril is fairly modest. She has two piercings in one ear and one in the other. She also opted for a more moderate belly button ring, rather than having any on her face or other risqué parts of her body. "I was gonna get one on my lip, but I decided not to because I think it would get in the way of kissing a guy. Plus, I'm thinking, Okay, when I'm 40, I don't want this huge hole in my lip. I would never do my tongue."

She also spoke extremely sensibly when it came to getting a tattoo, which until recently, she had none to speak of, saying, "I had so many tattoo ideas and I was like, 'Yeah, let's go do this now,' but then I'm like, 'Wait, be safe, think about it for a year and see if you still want it.' Then like two months later I'm like, 'Oh my God I'm so glad I didn't do it!'" However, she decided to take the plunge during the recording of her second album, when she and her friend/co-writer, Ben Moody, got matching star tattoos on their wrists. She has been seen with another tattoo as well, also on her wrist, of the letter 'D,' symbolizing her fiancé Deryck Whibley.

Besides her clothes, Avril's early look was supplemented by her dead-straight, honey-brown hair, which hung limp over her delicately featured face in a half rebellious, half shy girl manner. Her makeup was sparse, except around her eyes, which were outlined and re-outlined in large amounts of black eyeliner and mascara.

Avril always tries to surprise the photographers, and the press has come to expect the unexpected from her over the years. At the Grammy Awards in 2003, Avril's bandmates joined her in a quest to wear the most outrageous outfits at the ball. In a fashion review of the event on MTV.com, the title rings "Avril Gets Hideous" and goes on to describe the crazy costumes these kids had sported: "Rowdy and rag-tag Avril Lavigne and her band all wore the ugliest tuxedos they could find. On purpose. Lavigne wore a tux with studs and skull-and-crossbones…The rest of her bandmates wore clashing tuxes with gaggy water-squirting flowers and light-up bow ties." And what was her reason for wearing the flashy tux (that displayed the words "Rock On" when she opened the jacket)?

"There's no friggin' way I was going to wear a dress," she states in true Avril style.

The most significant part of her image, however, was her attitude, which she certainly wore on her sleeve, as well as on every other part of her body, and it resonated on stage and off, in rehearsal, in performance, in the studio and in person. For many of Avril's fans, her image was just as important as her music upon the release of her debut album. But even though her skater garb didn't always coincide with the poppy tunes she was belting out, the energy she exuded helped define her style and was a large piece of the puzzle in her becoming a worldwide superstar.

As explained in *Stylus* magazine, "she dresses like a real 17-year-old girl. Yeah, she wears skater clothes, and yeah, her music doesn't fit the scene, but she looks real cool and cute with that wife-beater and tie, baggy clothes and sneakers (all clothes you can buy at a local skate shop and not exclusive to Rodeo Drive)."

This combination of fashion, talent and attitude is what prevented people from looking the other way at her success. As another writer describes, "…what's not to love about her style? In her signature cargo pants and black chucks, she's dedicated to resisting frilly, hypersexual femminess, and to celebrating her adolescence."

Here was an average teenage girl with average teenage clothing who other average kids could relate to, but at the same time, she possessed an extraordinary talent that kids could also strive for, redefining and recreating the perfect teen idol.

negative press sucks

$Even$ with the cheering sounds of *Let Go* fans ringing throughout the world, it was only a matter of time before the press found something bad to say about Avril Lavigne. The release of the album during a pop-crazy era of manufactured artists also gave critics an easy route to take. Listeners began to attack her music and image as well, as a lot of people believed that she was simply another product of the recording industry. And since Avril had claimed a co-writership of the entire album, the public wondered how a 16-year-old newcomer could have had the knowledge to play an integral part in the creation of so many smash hits.

Something else that didn't help was that The Matrix songwriting team, which had guided Avril through a fantastic experience in Los Angeles, now alleged that their young collaborator actually had little input on her hit singles and that they had written the majority of the songs. "With those songs, we conceived the ideas on guitar and piano," said Lauren Christy. "Avril would come in and sing a few melodies, change a word here or there. She came up with a couple of things in 'Complicated,' like, instead of 'Take off your stupid clothes,' she wanted it to say 'preppy clothes.'" Seems like a rather ungrateful comment from a team who reportedly made $50,000 per song, four percent of album sales, and launched a flourishing career in songwriting from working with Avril.

While it remains a difficult concept to grasp—that the raw skills of a person so young could have made such an impact on the music industry—Avril explained her side of the story to *Rolling*

AvRiL tRiViA

In the *ChartAttack* Year-End Reader's Poll, Avril came out on top in the "Throw Your Underwear" category.

Stone magazine. "Me and Lauren sat down and wrote and did all the lyrics together for every single song. Graham would come up with some guitar stuff, and I'd be like, 'Yeah, I like that,' or 'No, I don't like that.' None of those songs aren't from me," she asserts.

Many use her age as an excuse to assume that the teenager could not possibly have an understanding of the kinds of things she claimed to have written about. She dressed like a punk and sang pop songs, and this kind of discrepancy must mean that she was not as smart as her record label made her out to be. Critics also bashed her so-called sellout to do more of a pop-rock sound when clearly she had grown up singing country music.

But Avril had many friends in high places backing her up, including Peter Zizzo, who was quick to endorse the teenager's achievement, saying, "Who of us at 15 had a completely clear picture of who we were? I think by doing something creative you find out who you want to be creatively. Avril was absolutely the architect of her record."

Even Nettwerk CEO, Terry McBride, finds an easy explanation for Avril's success and transformation from country to cultured. "When she was in Napanee, she was true to what Napanee was. She was a product of that environment," he begins. "But she's turned into a very worldly kid in a very short time. You plop that girl in New York City—where there are 5000 people in just one block—and you just put a kid in the candy store. Culture hit her over the head, and as with any teenager, it's like osmosis."

Avril goes on to defend her songwriting skills by describing where her inspiration came from. "When I wrote ['Complicated'], I was feeling what the song was about—that there are tons of people in the world who are fake, who are two-faced." She justifies her songwriting abilities as a gift, owing most of it to natural talent, saying, "Someone can say, 'Go write a song,' and I can do it. I can write a song a day." She adds, "Songwriting is like that for me," after stating that her debut single took only about two hours to write.

How much work Avril did and just how much The Matrix did we will never know, but the singer also alleges to have written "every single lyric and the melodies" for most of the tracks she created with Clif Magness, a claim that he has never refuted.

The feud was well documented by the press, which continued to have a go at her every chance they got, with one-sided views about bar fights, her clothes, her attitude, her music—anything they could find to bash, they did. Not only did the attacks come from noted members of the press, thanks to the Internet, but they also came from regular citizens. Would you believe that there is an entire "Anti-Avril" movement out there dedicated to criticizing everything about the young Canadian? One website states that its mission is "to convince you to become Anti-Avril while making you laugh…" Another says, "I mean, how can she claim to be a punk and a skater when she can't even skate?"

AvRiL tRiViA

Avril made the *FHM 100 Sexiest Women in the World* list from 2003 to 2005 inclusive, as well as being named one of the *Maxim Hot 100* in 2003 and 2005.

Too often condemned for her lack of punk music to accompany her punk-like image, Avril heartily responds, "I KNOW I'm not a punk...I never f***ing said I was!" Having also had skateboards spontaneously shoved in her face during interviews, she also angrily expresses her rebuttal to this erroneous assumption: "...because I once talked about how skateboarding was a big part of my life when I was younger, people found out and started asking me all these questions about it. Like I'm some Tony Hawk or something, which I'm not!"

Although Avril agrees that "negative press sucks," she understands that it goes along with the territory of being a celebrity, and there is little she can do about it. She is not quite content, however, to accept this reality just yet, as she ponders, "When you are in the public eye, you get labeled, and I just don't understand how people can label a human being, especially when they are young and growing and changing and evolving."

In an interview with *Reader's Digest*, she talks about how the media has portrayed her time and time again "as a punk, as a rebel, as a girl who is really angry." But Avril swears, "I'm just a girl who likes to rock out, to have fun, to let loose." One thing's for sure, whatever the critics say, we like to rock out, have fun and let loose with you, Avril!

under my skin: the album

With the incredible success of her debut album, and with the remaining skeptics on the prowl, the pressure was on for Avril Lavigne to deliver when it came to her sophomore release, *Under My Skin*, which hit stores on May 25, 2004. Because of the tension on the subject of her involvement in the writing of the songs on *Let Go*, many critics still believed that she was a product of a record company's strategic marketing and a professional writing team. Avril was determined to put these rumors to rest and take the destiny of her second album into her own hands.

While the team at Arista was anxious to get in on the action, the young singer claims that she "started the record before anyone even knew," and she did not even think about hinting to the record execs about what she was doing to prepare for the album. Basically, Lavigne locked herself away with her various collaborators and allowed no interference or guidance from anyone at her record label, which gave her the freedom she needed to grow and to find her own voice as a maturing young adult.

The first thing Avril chose to do in order to have full control of her record was to drop her previously successful songwriting team, The Matrix, from whom many of the negative rumors had stemmed. She found new collaborators in old and new friends, who were all notable musicians in their own right. Avril knew she could learn from them and mature as a writer in that kind of environment.

At a music industry party one night, fellow Canadian singer-songwriter Chantal Kreviazuk approached her. Avril had met Chantal before through her friend and Chantal's husband, Raine Maida, the lead singer of Our Lady Peace, who had opened for Avril on her first tour. Although Chantal and Avril were not close friends at the time, the songstress handed Avril her phone number and suggested that they "do lunch."

As Avril recalls, "She called me the next day and she was so adamant about going out. We ate, and we totally hit it off, and I was like, 'Do you want to write?'" A couple of days later, the two women got together and wrote a song. They knew immediately that there was something special in their collaboration and began writing incessantly. They continued to work for two weeks straight, writing a new song every single night. As Avril puts it, "We were on a major roll." No kidding!

Even though Chantal is older than Avril by a decade, the duo got along fantastically, and Avril was happy to be writing with another female, "'cause we'd sit there and be like, 'Yeah, guys do this!' and then write about it," she says. Kreviazuk, who is also managed by Nettwerk Records, is a classically trained pianist and award-winning singer/songwriter, and she was a great inspiration and mentor to Avril throughout the course of writing and recording *Under My Skin*. Avril even moved into Chantal and Raine's Malibu home for many months while they wrote and recorded the album. Maida also offered the use of his band's rehearsal space in Toronto for much of the writing. The space, Avril recalls, was a "big, old warehouse with mice. I was so nervous walking in. I remember holding my key when I'd go to my car, ready to poke somebody in the eyeball." Sounds charming.

But how do you stick a folky, lyrical pianist with a punky, raw and hard-edged teenager and expect songwriting success? As Lavigne explains, "...she'd be at the keyboard, and I'd be sitting there with my guitar. And she'd come up with some really pretty stuff and then I'd edge it up. Or I would come up with some harsh stuff and then she'd add hers." They must also both be night owls and chocolate lovers, since most of the writing sessions took place between midnight and 5:00 AM, accompanied by a variety of chocolate bars to carry them through.

Though perhaps an unlikely pairing, Avril found working with Chantal to be an extremely enjoyable and valuable experience for her, both professionally and personally, saying, "The cool thing about working with Chantal, was that she totally knew everything that I was going through at the time...It was very therapeutic for me. It was getting something out of me that was there." Chantal was certainly able to evoke a tremendous amount of emotion from her young apprentice, whose lyrics show a growing maturity and a positive divergence from her first album.

Besides Kreviazuk, Avril also collaborated with other noteworthy musicians on *Under My Skin*. Best friend and guitarist Evan Taubenfeld co-wrote three songs on the album. Ben Moody, former member of the popular, award-winning band Evanescence, also worked with Avril on one song (they have matching tattoos to prove it!).

As for producers, Avril hand-picked them, choosing Don Gilmore (who worked with the bands Good Charlotte and Linkin Park) and Butch Walker (formerly of Marvelous 3). Walker, an edgy musician who also took a hand in writing with Avril, later opened for her on the tour for the album. Raine Maida produced many of the tracks that resulted from Avril's collaborations with his wife, and he wrote one track with Avril as well.

> The personnel was not the only thing that Avril was determined to control in the making of her second album. She was also out to prove a point that she was an intelligent, industry-savvy 19-year-old who was capable of making the important decisions and playing an integral part in her music career.

"I'm so picky about *everything*," she explains about her involvement in multiple aspects of her album. "Right now I'm working on the album artwork. It's like, 'Send it back to me, make it a little darker here. Bring the border down, take the scratches off the photo.' I'm so into that." Avril was equally engaged in the designing of the merchandise that is sold at her shows and on her website.

Not only that, but she also took control of overseeing the sequencing and mastering of *Under My Skin*. "Sequencing" is the term used in the music industry for editing a recording using special software, and after all the sequencing is done, it is sent to a highly skilled sound engineer for "mastering." The engineer gets the recording ready for the public to hear and creates a final copy from which other copies can be made.

Avril says that working on the sequence for *Under My Skin* was not a walk in the park compared to the work done on *Let Go*. "You would not believe how much time I spent on the sequence,"

AvRiL tRiViA

Avril was nominated by PETA (People for the Ethical Treatment of Animals) as one of the sexiest vegetarians of 2005. Narrowly winning the title were *American Idol* Carrie Underwood and Coldplay's Chris Martin.

she exclaims. "I changed it over and over and over. The first record was so easy, I just sat down [and sequenced it]. With this one, I had it mastered three different times. I spent hours. I couldn't believe it myself. I'm crazy, but I got it perfect."

Well, Avril must have done something right, because after its May 2004 release, the album shot to number one in several countries, including the United States (where it sold more than 381,000 copies in its first week), the United Kingdom, Canada, Taiwan and Australia. Even after it dropped in the charts after a few weeks, it hit number one in Canada again, as well as returning to the top five in the United States and in many European countries, upon the release of the album's second single. In fact, *Under My Skin* went on to generate six singles!

How does Lavigne explain her successful instincts for her second album? "I was involved in every aspect of making this record. I'm very hands-on. I knew how I wanted the drums, the guitar tones and the structures to be. I under-stand the whole process so much better this time because I've been through it. I'm really picky with my sound."

Whatever she did, the critics seemed to like it. *BillBoard* magazine described her musical progress as having a "darker and more mature sound" and told listeners, "If her 2002 debut, *Let Go*, was for day, consider *Under My Skin* for night." E! Online also approved of the release, characterizing her work as containing "delightfully dour melodies, heartfelt lyrics and a still-solid pop sensibility."

So, what was this sound that the world could not seem to get enough of? It starts with the fast-moving track "Take Me Away," which sets the pace for the album right at the beginning. Avril and Evan co-wrote the song, and their young talent is evident immediately, setting a dark tone with its more rock-influenced edge. Quieter, more introspective verses contrast with clashing, abrasive guitars in the chorus and mirror the confusion in the lyrics, which talk about feeling lost and bewildered by a relationship and wanting to break free from those troubles. The song was released to Canadian rock radio as a radio-only single and then in Australia in 2005. Typical of the sound of a harder rock band, "Take Me Away" was produced by Don Gilmore, who had worked mainly with rock bands in the past, including Pearl Jam.

"Together," the second track on *Under My Skin,* is a little more delicate, aided by the gentle touch of Chantal Kreviazuk. Backed by Chantal's flowing arpeggios on the piano, the song is about an unraveled relationship with a boyfriend who doesn't make Avril feel very good about herself when she is around him. "When I'm alone I feel so much better, and when I'm around you I don't feel together," she sings. With the influence of Kreviazuk's beautiful melodies, "Together" shows a great deal of emotion and maturity. As *Words & Music* wrote, "the piano-driven 'Together' is a candid acknowledgment of a relationship gone south." Although not released as a single, the song is certainly a classy addition to the album and is one of Avril's favorites.

The next track, "Don't Tell Me," was the first single from the album and took the world by storm, going to number one all over the map, in Canada, Argentina, China and even on the Airplay World Official Top 100, which documents the "most popular singles on the radio compiled from a worldwide sample of 2650 top 40 radio playlist charts." It is a powerful song because it sends an important message to youth about not giving in to the pressure of having sex. Many viewed it as a pro-abstinence number, but Avril assures that it simply comes from the morals she learned from growing up in a Christian family. "I'm just saying, 'Have respect for yourself.' It's about being able to be strong and not letting a guy pressure you into doing something you don't want to do." She goes on to add, "I think it's important for young girls, because I think it's harder when you're younger."

> Taking this responsible stance came surprisingly early for Avril, who wrote "Don't Tell Me" with Evan when she was only 17, an endeavor that she found rewarding. "You know what I really like about that song, though?" she exclaims excitedly. "Evan wrote the guitar, and I wrote the rest of it, the lyrics and the melody. And I was only 17, and he was 18. Isn't that so cool? I'm really proud of me and him for that."

And so she should be, as the debut single sent her album straight to number one on the Billboard 200 and the U.K. Albums Chart within the first week of its release. "Don't Tell Me" was also certified gold in October 2004.

The fourth track and fourth single from the album, "He Wasn't," is probably the most spunky (and punky) song of the album. Surprisingly a co-write with Kreviazuk, the raging guitars and upbeat tempo definitely make this track a head banger. Simplistic in its theme, the lyrics portray the average teenage relationship perfectly: "I sit on my bed alone staring at the phone," and "This is when I start to bite my nails and clean my room if all else fails."

A song that could be described as "a bucket of fun," it maintains a kind of comic vibe throughout, which Avril emulates in her spoof-like video by prancing freely around on stage and at one point is even seen wearing a fairy costume! Although the single was not the most popular on the album, it still hit the top spot on the Canadian charts, making "He Wasn't" her eighth consecutive number one in her home country.

Next up on the album is a beautiful ballad, with an obvious influence by Ms. Kreviazuk, called "How Does It Feel." With a string arrangement by Avril, Raine and Chantal, the effortless melody is filled out by some talented string players, including Mark Robertson on violin (who has also played with such artists as Faith Hill, Hoobastank and Mary J. Blige), and Shanti Randall on viola (who is featured on albums with the likes of Ray Charles and Kelly Clarkson, and many movie soundtracks). During the bridge, Avril shows off her upper vocal range, sounding very much like one of her idols, Alanis Morissette. With heartfelt, thoughtful lyrics and elegant vocals, Avril shows her vulnerability with this sophisticated track.

The second smash hit of *Under My Skin* was "My Happy Ending," which hit radios in June 2004 and made its way to stores in August of that year. The song, which Avril co-wrote with Butch Walker, "...is about a breakup and me saying goodbye to all the memories," she explains. Because of its generic nature, the song easily relates to anyone who has ever had a relationship go sour after dreaming about a "happy ending." A well-constructed and engineered song, it returned *Under My Skin* to the top of the Canadian charts for several weeks, and back to the top five in the United Kingdom, the United States, Australia, Germany and a handful of other European countries. On the Billboard Hot 100, "My Happy Ending" peaked at number nine, and the RIAA certified it platinum in January 2005.

Arguably the most insightful song on *Under My Skin*, "Nobody's Home" was the third single from the album. Written about a girl Avril once knew, the song tells the story of a young woman who is emotionally lost in the world but doesn't know where to turn or how to accept help. Although the song was not very successful on the Billboard charts, it reached the number one spot in many countries and also received a great deal of airplay all around the world. Avril wrote "Nobody's Home" with former Evanescence member, Ben Moody, and it remains one of her most popular and significant songs to date.

Another song of the darker variety, "Forgotten" is a strong and aggressive ballad that shows the anger of someone who is ready to move on at the end of a relationship but has not forgotten the actions of the other. As *Words & Music* describes, Avril "takes an assertive stance with a boyfriend…[singing] over an accompaniment of classical strings." A collaboration with Kreviazuk, this powerful track commands the attention of the listener with its forceful lyrics and haunting melody.

"Who Knows" is a happier song about living life to the fullest and taking things as they come. Closer to the style of her first album, it is one of the more "poppy" songs on *Under My Skin*, but it maintains a kind of edginess, with harsher guitars and Avril's usual dynamic vocals. Perhaps not the strongest song on the album, it does add to the diversity of the record and continues to demonstrate the success of Lavigne and Kreviazuk's collaboration.

Although Raine Maida appears only once on the album as songwriter, he certainly gives a good showing with one of the prettiest songs on *Under My Skin*, with "Fall To Pieces." As the final single, the track did not get as much credit on the charts but still remains a favorite of fans around the globe. Entering the top 40 in the United States in mid-2005, the song took listeners by surprise with its soft melody and innate artistry. In Canada, this radio-only single was impressive enough to be given the number seven spot on the Canadian Top 20 of 2005. It is quite a feat to release a song almost an entire year after the release of the album, but Avril and Raine succeeded at creating a touching ballad about the complexities of an adult romance, once again showcasing Avril's growing maturity, as well as her incredible vocal range.

Back to showing a bit of youth, Avril teamed up with her band-mates Evan Taubenfeld and drummer Matt Brann to write "Freak Out." A lighthearted pop song in the end, the track opens with a hard-hitting guitar riff, but it quickly gives way to a more bubblegum-rock feel once the verse begins. With lyrics about being yourself, doing your best in life and letting things be, "Freak Out" shows a carefree side of Avril and her band. Evan especially shows his talents on this track, playing both electric and acoustic guitars and drums, and singing back vocals on the recording. Avril, who rarely rewrites anything that she has come up with, was not happy with "Freak Out" at first and decided to review the work. "I decided I didn't like the verses. I went back into the studio, and we had Evan put new guitars in, and I wrote all new melodies and lyrics….It doesn't happen very often, but it was worth it." It would be interesting to know what the original sounded like.

Living life in front of the world can be a difficult thing for a young celebrity like Avril, especially when she found out that her grand-father had passed away moments before going on stage for a show. She dedicated the performance to him but broke down and cried in front of a sympathetic audience. As a tribute to him because she was very close to her grandpa, Avril finished her album with the beautiful ballad, "Slipped Away," written with Chantal. The song is a sweet serenade backed by Kreviazuk on the piano, and Avril's voice combines a tender sadness and fragile desperation that evokes a lot of emotion for anyone who has ever lost some-one important to them. "Slipped Away" is a touching conclusion to a diversified and mature second album from Avril Lavigne.

The maturity of *Under My Skin* was well mirrored by our young Canadian rocker, who did not succumb to the pressures of the music industry, the media or the public, scoring big all around the globe with her second album. Throughout 2004, Avril filled her shelves with awards galore for her achievements with *Under My Skin*. At the World Music Awards on September 15, she was named the World's Best-Selling Canadian Artist and was also honored for doing what she does best by bridging the gap between pop and rock, winning the award for Best Pop Rock Artist.

She was also commended internationally at the Latin American MTV Video Music Awards with the title of Best International Pop Artist and similarly at Europe's NRJ Radio Awards in Cannes, France, as the Best International Female Artist. Her fans were equally pleased with her showing, selecting her as their Favorite Female Singer at the Nickelodeon Kids' Choice Awards, as well as dubbing her the People's Choice Favourite Canadian Artist at her country's own Much Music Video Awards.

The praise continued well into 2005 when she scored a hat trick at the 34th Annual Juno Awards held on April 3 at the MTS Centre in Winnipeg, Manitoba. Once again she gained the respect of her fans with the Juno Fan Choice Award but also cleaned up in the industry, winning the highly esteemed Artist of the Year Award and topping it off with a high five for Pop Album of the Year.

It was clear that the music-listening population was happy with the results of *Under My Skin*. Avril attributes the success of her second album to her vastly improved songwriting skills, which have advanced tremendously as she has gotten older. "This time around I feel like my songwriting had a lot more substance to it." She goes on, saying, "It was just deeper and a lot more personal because of my age and the way I express myself."

With such a varied collection of songs under her belt, it is safe to say that Avril's songwriting abilities come from a diverse set of influences, and she lists "The Beatles, the Beach Boys, Janis Joplin, Oasis, [and] Radiohead" as some of her favorite musicians. Understandably, she also cites Alanis Morissette as being one of her all-time idols, and it is easy to hear how her fellow Canadian has had an impact on her singing voice.

It also becomes obvious where much of the harsher sound on the album came from, as Avril points out that she listened to Marilyn Manson, Green Day and Blink-182 during the course of making the record. For *Under My Skin*, Avril reckons that she wrote close to 30 songs for the album before making the final cuts. "I didn't finish them all. I just kind of know if it's not going anywhere," she explains.

It is evident that Avril put a great deal of hard work and passion into the making of her second album, which has clearly paid off because *Under My Skin* was certified three times platinum by the Canadian Recording Industry Association in July 2004. Avril was now ready to take her show on the road.

get outta town

Selling millions of albums to fans all over the world is exciting for any artist, but it is the live connection that can be the most satisfying. Aside from being financially rewarding (most artists earn a small percentage from album sales, making a large portion of their earnings from touring), for musicians, there is nothing like the thrill of performing in front of a screaming audience, with bright lights shining in their eyes and doing what they most love to do, night after night.

Not only does Avril Lavigne enjoy the onstage part of touring, but she also loves the routine that develops from being on the road. "I'll finally be able to go to bed in the same place," she says with relief. She also explains that she prefers the tour bus, after experiencing a string of planes and hotels, saying, "The tour bus is like your home, your security. For the past nine months, I've been in a different bed every night, a different city. On the bus, it's like living in a house with your family."

Before setting off on her first performance tour, Avril had some practice in 2002 during a promotional excursion that, at one point, had her on 35 planes in 28 days! She quickly learned of the many downsides of touring, including "Lots of late nights." She spoke to *VH1* about her experience, pointing out that "Flights get in late, and by the time you check into your hotel room, unpack your toothbrush, brush your teeth, go to bed…and then you have to get up early in the morning—which is what it's been like for me lately—my body's just not used to it and it's getting worn down."

Living out of a suitcase is tough at the best of times, but how do musicians cope with all the demands of their hectic travel schedule when they are also expected to be in peak form in regards to their health? Avril, who described her throat as "getting kind of hoarse

AvRiL tRiViA

Avril's band doesn't record with her in the studio. She hires professional studio musicians to back her up, which is a common practice for solo artists, according to experienced producer Tom McKillip of Vancouver.

and raspy" during the 2002 promotional tour, took antibiotics to ease the soreness. It has been said that fellow Canadian, Céline Dion, avoids speaking for 24 hours before a live performance.

Avril also vowed, "I just need to try to stop talking and screaming and jumping around when I don't really need to." That can sometimes be difficult to accomplish with all of the media appearances and other temptations that go along with being a superstar.

Another sacrifice that Avril and other singers often have to make is to cut back on dairy, which is not good for the throat and voice. This is especially difficult for Avril because she loves pizza so much! "You know the sacrifice it is for me to live without pizza? I dream about pizza," she admits.

But it is all worth it in the end, because one thing's for certain, Avril loves performing live, and it shows in the energy she exudes on stage. After the amazing success of her first album, Avril undertook a most ambitious tour that started in the United States, took her around the world and then led her back to North America on a five-month, 41-show schedule. The tour, suitably named the Try To Shut Me Up tour, began on January 12, 2003, in Washington, D.C., and after two more American dates, proceeded to Singapore and then onto 17 cities throughout Europe and the United Kingdom. Finally, Try To Shut Me Up brought her

93

back to her home country, with eight Canadian stops, and she finished off the American leg of the tour with eight more cities, ending in Philadelphia on May 17. Phew! It sounds exhausting just thinking about it!

It's a good thing Avril got her health under control for this tour, because the tour certainly required that she exert a ton of energy each night. One concert reviewer who saw the show at the CSU Convocation Center in Cleveland described the night as "a 70-minute set that was met with teenage hysteria not heard since the early days of 'N Sync." During the course of the evening, Avril belted out 15 songs, including a surprise cover version of Green Day's "Basket Case."

She brought some other gifted Canadian musicians on tour with her, just to show the world what her rockin' home country was capable of. Accompanying her on the Try To Shut Me Up tour were veterans Our Lady Peace, who have been rocking stages since 1995, and Vancouver-based punk band, Gob, who had previously toured with Avril's buds from Sum 41 and were recently signed to Arista as well. This first tour turned out to be a great networking experience for Avril. She became close friends with the members of both bands and later found a new bass player in Craig Wood of Gob, as well as collaborators in Raine Maida and his wife, Chantal Kreviazuk.

Avril's live success was documented in *My World*, a DVD recording of her show in Buffalo, New York. The recording included

AvRiL tRiViA

Avril named her second worldwide tour the "Bonez" tour because bones are, she says, "under my skin."

rare behind-the-scenes footage of the thriving tour, as Avril played to sold-out crowds all over the world, sky-rocketing her fame from radio sensation to real-life rock star.

Her second tour was more low key than the first. With the goal of promoting her sophomore album, *Under My Skin*, Avril set off on a whirlwind 21-city tour. But this was not just your average tour. Gone were the days when pop stars, such as the multi-platinum selling '80s singer Tiffany, stormed a local mall and dazzled their screaming fans on a makeshift stage in center court—or were they? Actually, Avril Lavigne's label decided to do just that.

In each of the 21 North American cities, the show was announced on the radio, and fans who had registered on Avril's official web-site were sent an e-mail about the surprise stop. Her fans had 48 hours to get their butts down to the local shopping mall, where they could see a free acoustic performance by Avril and her main guitar guy, Evan Taubenfeld. The duo performed a 30-minute set that included seven songs, giving listeners a taste of what was to come from her soon-to-be-released album.

Generating what one journalist called a "small stampede" of "Avrilophiles," this approach was a great way for the superstar to connect with her fans and to showcase her genuine talent without the ruckus of a band behind her. "I love it," Avril said of the acoustic experience. "I'm doing it to show people I can play and sing. It's stripped down and intimate. When I'm playing with a band it's harder. There's so much f****** noise, and you're wearing ear monitors."

> The spur-of-the-moment tour didn't seem to bother the fans, who seemed to find ways of coming out despite the short notice. "The last couple shows were 10,000 kids, so we had to move outside. We're suppose to be playing inside the mall." Guess the mall tour idea isn't dead yet!

Of course this was not the only tour Avril undertook surrounding the release of *Under My Skin*. Falling under the title of the Bonez tour, she embarked on another world tour, but this time for only three months, and went on a second North American leg the following summer. The first section started in Munich, Germany, on September 26, 2004, with stops in the United Kingdom, Europe, the United States, and finally, Canada, finishing on November 25 in the beautiful city of Kelowna, British Columbia. Avril also regained the world tour with six dates in Australia in May 2005, and a stop in Johannesburg, South Africa, where she played to a crowd of 20,000 at the Coca-Cola Dome.

Opening for her this time was seasoned performer Butch Walker and pop-punk band American Hi-Fi. The second part of the Bonez tour remained in North America, hitting up a few of the same locations as before but adding a bunch more, covering 22 cities. Starting in London, Ontario, on July 13, 2005, Avril made the rounds, once again followed by Butch Walker and also new-comer Gavin DeGraw, ending up at Montreal's Bell Centre on September 3.

Even though touring can be exhausting, with its grueling schedule and crazy fans, Avril feels very much at home when she's on tour. "I'll be waking up on the bus. I want to get a routine going; do some walking, do some alone time, read, cook. If I do that, and I have a show, I'll feel better." Walking, reading and cooking. So that's what the life of a rock star is like.

calling for backup

Although it is Avril's name that we scream at her concerts, her voice that we hear on the radio and her face that we see in music news all over the world, the truth is, she would not be so energetic and inspiring on stage if not for the fabulous band that backs her up. "I'm a solo artist and it's my name, but I have the band vibe, and I want people, when they hear my name or think 'Avril Lavigne,' to think of me and the guys…That's how much I want them to be involved in this," Avril explains.

"The Band" has fluctuated since its conception but still remains a strong force in Avril's sound. So how do you choose the band for a hard-edged female firecracker like Avril Lavigne? Her manager, Shauna Gold, fills us in: "She's young, her music's young, we needed a band that would fit well with who she is as a person… Maybe they're not top-of-the-line studio musicians, but they still play really well and have the right energy and the right look."

The current evolution of the band has Matt Brann as drummer, Charlie Montiz as bassist, Devon Bronson on lead guitar and Craig Wood on rhythm guitar. Matt Brann was born in Ajax, Ontario, on November 14, 1980. If you're thinking, "that town sounds familiar," you're right. Ajax is the home of the guys from Sum 41. In fact, Matt went to Exeter High School with Jason McCaslin, also known as "Cone," the bassist from Sum 41, and the two played together in a band called Second Opinion. Matt and Cone were actually so close that people called Matt "Cone 2"! Matt remains close with Cone and also with Sum 41 manager

AvRiL tRiViA

Avril and her band toured the nation in the bus
of the hardcore band, KoRn.

Greig Nori (from Treble Charger), who actually thanked Matt on
the album *Detox*. Matt is said to be a big fan of Madonna, Pink
and, of course, Avril!

Charlie Moniz has been with
Avril's band since September
2002. Born on October 31, 1982,
in Burlington, Ontario, Charlie
used to be the drummer in a
band called Grade, who released
one album, *Headfirst Straight To
Hell*, with Victory Records in
2001. He was friends with Matt
before joining Avril and wanted
very much to be in the band. So
much, in fact, that because the
position of drummer was already
taken, he changed instruments,
and has been the band's bassist
ever since. His favorite band is
The Clash, and he was a great
addition to the band as he has
been playing punk music since
he was eight years old. Like his
buddy Matt, Charlie is a big fan
of Pink, and also has a bit of a
crush on Vanessa Carlton.

Possibly the sexiest position in any band's history is the lead guitar. Held by Evan Taubenfeld for many years, the position is now filled by Devon Bronson. Devon is the only American in the band, his hometown being Santa Clarita, California. He has, however, played with a Canadian band in the past as a member of Treble Charger but is most known for his brief stint as rhythm guitarist with Kelly Osbourne. Daughter of the legendary Ozzy Osbourne from the rock band Black Sabbath, Kelly was dropped from her record label almost as soon as she was signed, after releasing a revival of Madonna's "Papa Don't Preach." Devon also used to be in a band called NEO, and his first appearance with Avril's band was on September 16, 2004, at the World Music Awards.

On rhythm guitar is Torontonian Craig Wood. Craig was a member of the band Gob, who opened for Avril on her Try To Shut Me Up tour. Although he played bass with Gob, Craig was also proficient on the guitar and was eager to join Avril's band when Jesse Colburn left. Craig's first show with the band was in 2004 at the Juno Awards. "…he's great. It was cool because we already knew him, and we'd already toured with him," said Lavigne about Craig.

What does Avril have to say about her band? "We have something really special, and we connect really well. It's strange, but it really feels like we're all supposed to be together. It's like a really cool, unique situation." Well, they weren't all meant to be together, indicated by the number of former band members that have said goodbye over the last few years.

Mark "London" Spicoluk was the original bass player for Sum 41 and quite good friends with the band until Cone replaced him in the band and they all lost touch. Mark was the original bassist for Avril's band but left in September 2002 (replaced by Charlie Moniz) to continue playing in the punk band Closet Monster. Like Sum 41, the guys from Closet Monster are from Ajax, Ontario, and Spicoluk played bass for the band, as well as being the lead vocalist. Although the group split after their Christmas show in 2005, they remain amicable with their bandmates. Mark is the head honcho of his own independent record label, Underground Operations, which is based out of Toronto, and now works with seven different acts in the punk music domain, including Closet Monster, which was their most successful act.

Mark Spicoluk introduced Jesse Colburn to Avril, and they were quick to form a connection. Avril and Jesse got along so well that they reportedly became a couple very quickly. Born on May 5, 1981, in Ajax, Ontario, Colburn is three and a half years older than Avril, and he played rhythm guitar for her band from its inception, right up until March 2004, when he supposedly left for personal reasons. Despite many presuming that his departure was due to an interband love gone sour, Avril insists, "He just wanted to go do his own thing and stuff, and I mean, that happens." Jesse has played in several bands, including AWOL, The Oisters, Sulpher, and most recently, Closet Monster with Mark Spicoluk. In fact, Jesse was the band member who posted Closet Monster's announcement that their 2005 Christmas show would be their last.

Probably the saddest departure from Avril's band was when her best friend and lead guitar, Evan Taubenfeld, left the band. Evan connected with Avril through one of his Spinfire bandmates who was working at Arista at the same time the young Canadian songstress was signed to the label. Evan flew to New York especially to audition for the band and was selected that same night. Originally from Baltimore, Maryland, Evan is the closest to Avril in age, born on June 27, 1983. When he was just two years old, Evan's parents bought him a Sesame Street drum set for Hanukkah. He soon picked up a guitar and started his first band, called Spinfire, in high school. The band broke up in 2002 because they had tried to do five shows a week, which kept them up until 3:00 AM, and they had to be in class a few hours later at 7:00 AM. This proved to be too much for the young group, but it worked out for Evan, as he joined Avril's band later that year. Twice accepted to the prestigious Berklee College of Music in Boston (once for drums and once for guitar), Evan opted to follow Avril instead, a decision he probably does not regret. Not only are Avril and Evan best of friends on and off the stage, but they are also a great songwriting duo, having teamed up for several songs on *Under My Skin.*

In 2004, however, Evan decided to pursue his own musical goals rather than join Avril on her Bonez tour and was replaced by Devon Bronson. Evan is now signed by Sire Records and will release an album very soon, having now officially moved to Los Angeles. Even though she misses her best bud, Avril doesn't have any negative feelings about Evan's decision, saying, "He had wanted for a long time to start his own band. After recording the album, he decided to dedicate himself fully to that project, and so he didn't have time to come on tour with me. I'm not at all opposed to his decision. That said, it is very probable that we will collaborate again one day." We hope so!

hurray for hollywood

Apart from her two albums, Avril's voice has also graced the big screen, making contributions to several movie soundtracks. Her first movie venture came in September 2002 in the movie *Sweet Home Alabama*. For this popular romantic comedy, Avril sang "Falling Down," a song that was originally rejected from *Let Go* and was a result of her collaboration with The Matrix. Suitable for this movie, the song actually sounds more like pop-country, which is probably why it was cut from the album, but it can be found in Avril's collection of B-sides (unreleased tracks).

In 2003 Avril's next opportunity arose when she supplied an original song for the *American Wedding* (*American Pie 3*) soundtrack, along with other notable artists such as the Wallflowers, Sum 41, the Foo Fighters, the All-American Rejects and Good Charlotte. Avril was one of the few female additions to the soundtrack, and her funky, '80s pop-influenced track, "I Don't Give," adds a nice taste of "Avril attitude" to the disc.

Following *American Wedding*, Avril became involved in the *Princess Diaries 2: Royal Engagement* soundtrack in 2004. On this album, Avril performed the song "I Always Get What I Want," which brings down the house with its hardcore punk guitars. It could easily be a Green Day song if it weren't for Avril's screaming, yet silky, voice. Not only did Avril provide the song, but she also co-wrote the Kelly Clarkson track, "Breakaway," which ended up as the title track to Kelly's second album (and incidentally, won the 2006 Grammy Award for Best Pop Vocal Album).

The single was so successful for Clarkson that it held the Number One spot on the Billboard Adult Contemporary chart for 21 non-consecutive weeks!

Probably the most fun of all of Avril's soundtrack projects was when she had the honor of singing the theme song for the popular *The SpongeBob SquarePants Movie*, which was released in late 2004. With a catchy chorus that sings, "Who lives in a pineapple under the sea? SpongeBob SquarePants!," the fun-filled song was arranged by Avril with the help of co-writer and producer Butch Walker. "I made the song a little more edgy," said Lavigne, who recorded the theme during the course of her demanding tour schedule. "It's kind of like the rock version of [the original]. There are a lot of loud guitars, and we picked the tempo up a little and sang it with a little more attitude." Joining Avril on the soundtrack were The Flaming Lips and, of course, SpongeBob himself.

Not only has Avril's singing voice made its way into films, but her speaking voice is also expected to make its debut as the voice of Heather in the animated flick *Over the Hedge*, set to release on May 19, 2006. Besides a few cameo appearances in 2004, one in the movie *Going the Distance* and another on the TV show, *Sabrina, the Teenage Witch*, her role in *Over the Hedge* will be Avril's first go at acting.

Over the Hedge is based on a popular comic strip by the same name, created by Michael Fry and T. Lewis, which views suburban living through the eyes of the animals that first inhabited the area. Avril plays the daughter of Ozzie the Possum (voiced by William Shatner) in this intelligent cartoon that follows RJ the Raccoon and his best friend Verne the Turtle as they "fight to save their wooded wonderland from the evils and temptations of encroaching suburbia…but end up becoming distracted by wide-screen TVs, discarded fast food, comfy lawn furniture and the fun of wreaking havoc with the local homeowners' association."

Avril is accompanied by a star-studded cast in *Over the Hedge*, including Bruce Willis, Garry Shandling, Eugene Levy, Allison Janney, Nick Nolte and Catherine O'Hara. Here's what Avril says about her first professional acting experience: "My part's pretty

AvRiL tRiViA

small so it was easy enough, but it was my first ever film…It was easier because it was just voiceover, so I didn't have to be on camera, and it was fun. It's my voice, and I'm just supposed to be young, and my dad embarrasses me a lot."

So how did all this acting business come about? As Avril explains, "I was on tour for a year, and I started thinking about what I wanted to do next. I wanted to start doing fashion and acting." In 2005 she signed with International Creative Management, one of the largest literary and talent agencies in the world, with offices in New York, London and Los Angeles. "I want to do this for a bit of a change… I want to start off small, see how I like it and make sure I'm comfortable."

Besides her experience with the Lennox Community Theatre as a child, Avril does not have any acting training, but like the self-starter she is, she says, "I'm just reading the script and acting out how I think it should be." Avril knows she needs to proceed with caution in her singer-turned-actor attempts, "because when you're a singer, acting can be…well, cheesy," she admits.

While she may be proceeding cautiously, she is still moving full-speed ahead and already finished filming her second movie in New Mexico at the end of 2005. This time we will actually get to see Avril (as opposed to just hearing her) as she shares the screen with the likes of Richard Gere and Claire Danes in the crime-drama, *The Flock*. In this independent film, Gere plays a federal agent who is investigating the connection between a missing girl and a paroled sex offender. He questions a young man whose girlfriend (played by Lavigne) also has to answer a few questions herself. For the small part, Avril had a makeover, complete with glasses and a chipped tooth! "…I had to get a mold of my mouth so they could fit a (fake) chipped tooth," she laughed.

Next up for Lavigne is a slightly meatier role in the Richard Linklater (*School of Rock*) movie, *Fast Food Nation*, based on the 2001 bestseller by award-winning journalist Eric Schlosser. The book was first serialized for *Rolling Stone* magazine in 1999 and was transformed into a fascinating book that picks apart the fast-food industry in the United States. The film, set for release sometime in 2006, is a fictional adaptation of Schlosser's book, rather than following the documentary route, as was done in the 2004 release of the controversial *Super Size Me*. Avril plays a fast-food clerk in *Fast Food Nation*, along with a stellar cast that includes Wilmer Valderrama (who plays "Fez" on *That '70s Show*), Greg Kinnear and Ethan Hawke. This "burgers and fries" tale should be an interesting experience for Avril, who is actually a vegetarian!

Though there is no news right now about anymore of Avril's acting endeavors, we certainly look forward to seeing her on the big screen!

little woman

While her early image acted as a way to reel in her fans from all over the world, Avril is growing up, and her fame is beginning to reach heights beyond anything imaginable. Changes in her appearance have become more and more evident since the release of her second album. Although she may still maintain a similar down-to-earth outlook, it is obvious that she has grown into a young woman who is enjoying the luxuries of stardom.

In the last couple of years, her jeans have become increasingly more fitted (though still not reaching the painted-on look of many of the queens of pop) and her tops more feminine. Despite the expected bombardments from the press, Avril has been open with interviewers when asked about her recent transformation, saying, "Now I'm into skirts. I'm growing up, I'm changing, I'm becoming a woman. That happens to girls—they become women."

If her quote is not enough to tell you that her look is in a state of flux, you only need to glimpse the cover of the magazine that published the interview. Avril posed for the cover of the men's mag, *Maxim*, wearing a tightly squeezing black bustier top! Her hair, hanging almost down to her waist, is styled in kinky waves and shows off her new blonde and black hair extensions.

She also graced the cover of *Cosmopolitan* magazine in 2005 in a similar black top, looking absolutely stunning with her newly bleached, honey-blonde hair, which demonstrates the full extent of her morph from girl to woman. Now with curls and waves flowing in every direction, wearing provocative, peachy lip gloss and a noticeable lack of the usual black nail polish, Avril has definitely turned over a new leaf as far as her image is concerned.

AvRiL tRiViA

On May 6, 2003, Avril honored one of the legends of rock music by joining a stellar cast for Metallica's *MTVIcon* tribute. She sang the song, "Fuel," a track from the band's 1997 album, *ReLoad*.

Though her tastes are undeniably changing, her onstage persona appears to preserve many of her old stylistic characteristics, while incorporating some new ones at the same time. On one "interactive youth" website, a writer describes Avril from a concert on her latest tour: "Reigning Avril Lavigne came on in full golden-blond, layered-locked glory, in a black Dickies T-shirt, black tight jeans and silver belt chains." A good description of Avril, old and new!

For those of you who were in love with Avril's former skater look, you needn't be too concerned, as she has held on to her vintage T-shirts and has been spotted on stages all over the world wearing looser-fitting pants. She also continues to wear a variety of clunky combat boots and, of course, still sports her favorite (and ours!) classic Converse sneakers.

Always managing to blow away onlookers with her next move in fashion, music or otherwise, Avril's ultimate transformation in her look occurred only recently, and it succeeded in shocking people worldwide. In the February 2006 issue of *Harper's Bazaar* magazine, the Canadian pop rocker is featured in an article titled "Avril Lavigne Remixed," which outlines a side of her that fans never expected in a million years. Displaying what has been called her "china-doll precise" features, Avril adorns the pages of *Bazaar* in $3000 and $4000 dresses made by Gucci and Chanel, which must be a size zero, at the most, in order to fit snuggly over her teeny tiny frame. Still bearing her signature dark colors (namely black and midnight blue), the dresses came complete with puffy sleeves and Manolo Blahnik pumps. The clothes were complemented by her porcelain skin and silky, golden hair, which was neatly tied back into a sophisticated low ponytail and draped carefully over one shoulder.

> The most surprising of the outfits (which she got to pick out from an array of clothing) was an Yves Saint Laurent skirt suit in which she sinuously poses with no less than a $2000, flowing, off-white blouse. Avril in a blouse? No way! Even she couldn't believe her eyes, as she said, "Oh, my God...I look so Fifth Avenue," upon seeing a Polaroid picture of herself during the shoot.

And what does the punk-turned-princess have to say about all of these changes? "I'll look back at [old] pictures and think, "I was such a little tough-ass...I'm starting to feel more feminine. I'm getting into hair and makeup and image. That's the best part about being a girl." So much for the antifashion Avril of yore.

This new "high-fashion" Avril seemingly emerged after she received a Prada bag as a gift. She then bought an infamous Burberry followed by a Louis Vuitton. So she was stocked up as far as designer labels go, but this acquisition of fancy bags also sparked a little more inspiration for Avril than simply having a place to keep her lip balm and keys. After conquering the world, one song at a time, she decided to broaden her skills and expand the diversity of her abilities. Following the photo shoot with *Bazaar*, it was quite obvious to all that modeling was to be one of her developing talents.

> In the *Bazaar* interview, Avril revealed that she had signed with Ford Models and had plans to pursue the activity professionally, with a specific interest in high fashion. "I want to do those really beautiful ads with the high-end products," she explains.

The company that signed her will no doubt help her in achieving this goal. Ford Models, which was founded in 1964 by Eileen and Jerry Ford, is one of the most renowned and respected modeling agencies in the world. Over the years it has represented an amazing number of modeling superstars, such as Christie Brinkley and Twiggy (seen on *America's Next Top Model*), and Nigel Barker (mostly known currently as the handsome photographer also on *ANTM*).

Avril will be in good company, as Ford also represents a number of other celebrity models, including Courtney Cox, Mya and Lindsay Lohan. While modeling is still a brand new endeavor for the singer, Avril remains confident about her abilities: "I look through the magazines and stare at the ads and think, 'I'm not six feet tall, but I can do that.'"

And so, instead of seeing her strut down the red carpet at award shows this year, Avril Lavigne can be spotted at fashion events worldwide. On February 1, 2006, Avril was seen at Fashion Week in Paris at the Chanel Haute Couture Show, fully clad in—what else—a beautiful black Chanel dress. Apparently heading to Chanel designer Karl Lagerfeld's couture show, the platinum blonde bombshell even received a tour of Coco Chanel's home! Avril was also photographed for the February 4th issue of *Us Weekly* magazine, and the caramel-colored, leather trench coat that fits perfectly over her miniscule silhouette leaves nothing of the old skater girl image in our minds.

From skater to sensational, and punk to picturesque, it is obvious that Avril Lavigne has been a fashion icon from the second she stepped into the spotlight in 2002. Whether she meant to or not in her early days, she spawned new trends, carried on old ones in legendary style, and gave her fans an achievable look to aspire to. Although her new high-fashion image may be a little less reachable for fans than it was in previous years, we can be assured that Avril will remain on the forefront of fashion and be a visual attraction for the public throughout her continuously accelerating career.

chapter eighteen

a heart of gold, black and red

It's clear that Avril Lavigne certainly doesn't seem to worry about saying the wrong thing. She also stands up for herself in the face of criticism from others in the industry. In a newsworthy feud with fellow singer/actor, Hilary Duff, Avril held her own when Duff disapproved of the way she acted towards her tie-wearing, copycat fans.

In an interview with *Newsweek*, Avril rebutted, saying, "I read that I was supposedly mad at my fans for dressing like me...They quoted Hilary Duff saying, 'Avril needs to appreciate her fans more and blah, blah, blah.' I'm like, excuse me? First off, it's not even true. I never said that. And second, who the hell cares what she has to say about my fans? Whatever. Hilary Duff's such a goody-goody, such a mommy's girl."

Although Lavigne had never met Hilary Duff, her statement caught everyone a little off guard and generated a bit of a media frenzy, as she went on to say about Duff, in a mocking tone, "...I'm sure she's really nice and really sweet. I'm sure she's all smiles."

The feud continued when Avril allegedly bashed Duff once more in the *New York Daily News* in which she declared, "I don't really like her...I can tell what she's like...She's too much of a kiss-ass. You can tell that she's a goody-goody...She'll probably try to avoid me for the rest of her life." One Boston newspaper even reported that she ripped a photo of Duff off the wall during an interview at a radio station, accompanying the act with several expletives. For some reason it remains difficult to find any kind of

AvRiL tRiViA

Avril was disgusted when she learned that Ashlee Simpson had lip-synched on *Saturday Night Live*, saying, "I know for a fact there are some young female artists who don't even sing on their own records and who don't sing live. And that is pathetic....I've never lip-synched once."

retort from Miss Duff. All that aside, it appears that the feud between Avril and Hilary has cooled. According to Avril's manager, Shauna Gold of Nettwerk, the two are actually now friends.

Still opinionated and uncensored, Avril is not afraid to share her point of view. She is also quick to pass judgment on Britney Spears, ridiculing her dress style: "I mean, the way she dresses—would you walk around in a f*****' bra?"

Avril is known for saying some pretty controversial things at times, and you would think that her public relations team would cringe at some of the statements she makes. But as Mark Jowett assures about Nettwerk, "We're not a company that guides or coaches people on what they should say and not say…it's important that our [artists] feel that they can be themselves and speak, show their audience who they are really." He goes on to say, "They're also people, you know, so we try not to censor our artists, and rarely do we have to…I think if we tried to censor it, somehow it probably would come out in a different way, probably worse somehow."

It's a good thing Nettwerk feels that way, or they might have to hire someone full time to follow the headstrong Avril around with a censor button!

On the opposite end of the spectrum, something that Nettwerk is proud of, is Avril's unwavering dedication to various charitable causes. After all, regardless of the petty conflicts with other celebrities (and despite how much black she wears), Avril Lavigne has a heart of gold and understands that there are more important issues in the world than her own. Involved in several ongoing charities, she is a known activist in many areas.

Under the umbrella of the United Nations Association's Adopt-A-Minefield Campaign, Avril and many of her fellow artists have joined Paul McCartney's movement, Music Clearing Minefields. The campaign "uses the power of music…to support mine-clearing efforts around the world" by donating VIP concert tickets, exclusive "meet and greets" and other amazing opportunities that are auctioned on the Charity Folks website.

For the U.S. Campaign for Burma, Avril donated her song "Complicated" for use on the CD release, *For the Lady*, along with other artists such as U2, R.E.M., Bonnie Raitt, Sting, Ben Harper and Coldplay. The proceeds from the album sales go towards the campaign's mission "to free the world's only imprisoned Nobel Peace Prize recipient Aung San Suu Kyi (pronounced Ong Sawn Sue Chee) and all people in the Southeast Asian country of Burma."

The largest wish-granting organization in the world, the Make-A-Wish Foundation, is one of the most well-known charities around. Avril has participated in the organization by donating concert tickets and backstage passes that are auctioned for the cause.

In April 2003 Avril sang a cover of Bob Dylan's classic, "Knocking on Heaven's Door," on the benefit CD, *Peace Songs*. She is joined by such artists as David Usher, Bryan Adams, Our Lady Peace and David Bowie, and the proceeds from the CD's sales go to War Child Canada, which "works with young Canadians and the music industry to educate and raise awareness and support for war-affected children everywhere." Avril is featured on the website sporting a War Child tank top and is said to be "an ongoing, dedicated supporter of the charity."

In May 2003 Avril also united with fellow Canadians Sarah McLachlan, Remy Shand, Glenn Lewis, Sum 41 and the Barenaked Ladies to perform at the Concert for Toronto, a benefit concert in support of the city's economic battle due to the SARS outbreak. The performers gathered in two different venues, Air Canada Centre and the adjacent Skydome, and were video linked so that their fans could see all the action. Seventy-thousand tickets went in three hours, selling out the event!

Avril's most recent charity venture, just announced in December 2005, has her joining with others for the Amnesty International movement called Make Some Noise. The campaign, which launched on December 10 (International Human Rights Day), "aims to inspire a new generation to celebrate and stand up for human rights," by having popular artists perform songs by the great John Lennon. Singles and a compilation album will both be available to download online, starting with tracks by artists such as The Black Eyed Peas and Maroon 5. Songs by Avril (she sings the amazing and memorable "Imagine") and other artists will be available for download sometime in 2006, with profits from the sales going towards the organization's mission to promote global human rights.

AvRiL tRiViA

Avril had the privilege of performing in the closing ceremonies of the 2006 Torino Winter Olympic Games in Italy. She sang "Who Knows," a song that represented the transition towards the 2010 Games in Vancouver, BC.

Lastly, Avril is also currently an advocate of Aldo Fights Aids, which is a collaboration between the Aldo Shoes company and YouthAIDS. Avril is featured on the main page of the website, alongside the powerful quote, "Be strong, stand up, make a difference." The campaign, which is fronted by Avril and over two dozen other celebrities, raises funds by selling "empowerment tags" with the word "HEAR" on them. One hundred percent of the proceeds go into the development and implementation of AIDS/HIV prevention and education programs worldwide.

Besides sharing her heart with so many worthwhile charities, Avril also has a special cause in her personal life that takes up much of her attention. After years of being good friends with the guys from Sum 41, Avril finally admitted to having a relationship with the band's lead singer, fellow Ontarian, Deryck Whibley. At no more than 5' 5", he is the perfect match (and height!) for Avril, with his punky style and attitude. The two bought a house together in California, and after reportedly dating since early 2004, Avril and Deryck got engaged in January 2005.

Although Avril won't discuss her personal life, Harper's *Bazaar* reports, "her eyes light up even as she refuses to talk about him." Wearing a massive five-carat diamond ring on her finger, Avril says that she has already hired a wedding planner. She also has an idea of what she wants to wear and says that she now needs someone to design it for her. With Avril being only 21 years of age and Deryck only 25, many people have commented that they are both very young to be considering marriage already. However, Avril assures, "Everything has come superfast for me, a lot faster than for most people. I don't have the average lifestyle. I just know in my heart that I'm doing the right thing."

Avril is continuously working on material for a third album, but she is so busy pursuing new interests in acting and fashion that it is not surprising she has not yet set a date for its release. "Don't expect the album any time soon," she says. "I'm going to get off the road, take my time, be with my little sweetheart and have a life—and then get back to business."

While Avril fans all over the world are starving for hot new music from their favorite singing superstar, at least they can catch a glimpse of her as she makes her mark in different areas of the Hollywood scene. Signed with International Creative Management and Ford Models, Avril will try her luck on the on the big screen and on the catwalk for a bit until we hear her again on the radio.

One thing is certain, Avril Lavigne's potential is limitless, not only in the music industry, but also on whatever else she chooses to focus her talents. Quiet confidence, rebellious grace, a hard-edged romantic and a heartwarming activist— all could be used to describe her multifaceted persona as it continues to evolve and dominate the world of music, and persist in surprising a growing number of onlookers.

Blessed with the voice (and face) of an angel, a good head on her shoulders and a determination second to none, Avril Lavigne is poised for a career with longevity, dignity and many adoring fans. With Avril having already accomplished so much in the last five years, the scary part is, it looks as though she's just getting started.

discography

Let Go

Released: June 4, 2002 (North America)
Chart Position: Number two in the U.S.

Singles:

2002: "Complicated," "Sk8er Boi," "I'm With You"
2003: "Losing Grip," "Mobile"

Under My Skin

Released: May 25, 2004 (North America)
Chart Position: Number one in the U.S.

Singles:

"Don't Tell Me"
"My Happy Ending"
"Nobody's Home"
"He Wasn't"
"Fall to Pieces"

filmography

The Flock (2006)

Fast Food Nation (2006)

Over the Hedge (voice of Heather) (2006)

Going the Distance (as herself, cameo) (2004)

Sabrina, the Teenage Witch (TV show – as herself, guest star) (2oo4)

awards & nominations

2002

MTV Music Video Award
New Artist in a Video for "Complicated"

MTV Music Video Award Latin
Best International New Artist

World Music Awards
Best Canadian Pop/Rock Artist

Grammy Awards Nominations
Song of the Year: "Complicated"
Best Female Pop Vocal Performance: "Complicated"
Best Pop Vocal Album: *Let Go*
Best Rock Vocal Performance - Female: "Sk8er Boi"
Best New Artist

2003

Juno Awards
Best Single: "Complicated"
Best New Artist
Best Pop Album: *Let Go*
Best Album of the Year: *Let Go*
Ivor Novello Award
International Hit of the Year: "Complicated"

Juno Awards Nominations
Songwriter of the Year
Fan Choice Award

Radio Music Award
Song of the Year (Modern Adult Contemporary
  Radio): "Complicated"

Grammy Awards Nominations
Best Female Pop Vocal Performance
Song of the Year - Songwriter: "I'm With You"
  (with The Matrix)
Best Rock Vocal Performance Female: "Losing Grip"

American Music Awards Nomination
Favorite Pop/Rock Female Artist

2004

World Music Awards
Best Pop/Rock Artist
World's Bestselling Canadian Artist

MTV Video Music Award Latin America
Best International Pop Artist

Nickelodeon Kids' Choice Awards Nomination
Favourite Female Singer

Much Music Video Award
People's Choice Favourite Canadian Artist

NRJ Radio Music Award
Best International Female Artist

MTV Video Music Awards Nomination
Best Pop Video: "Don't Tell Me"

American Music Awards Nomination
Favorite Pop/Rock Female Artist

Juno Awards Nominations
Music DVD of the Year
Fan Choice Award

2005

Juno Awards
Artist of the Year
Pop Album of the Year: *Under My Skin*
Fan's Choice Award

Juno Awards Nominations
Songwriter of the Year
Album of the Year: *Under My Skin*

Notes on Sources

Books

Blum, Charlotte. *Avril Lavigne: de A à Z.* Paris: Groupe Express Editions. 2005.

Thorley, Joe. *Avril Lavigne: The Unofficial Book.* London: Virgin Books Ltd. 2003.

Tracy, Kathleen. *Avril Lavigne.* Delaware: Mitchell Lane Publishers. 2005.

Magazines

Brown, Laura. "Avril Lavigne Remixed." *Harper's Bazaar,* February 2006: 212–215.

Chorney-Booth, Elizabeth. "Avril Lavigne: Independent Woman." *Chart,* June 2004: 28–32.

Deziel, Shanda. "Avril Lavigne (Profile)." *Maclean's,* 13 January 2003: 22–27.

Eliscu, Jenny. "Little Miss Can't Be Wrong." *Rolling Stone,* 20 March 2003: 38–42.

Jennings, Nicholas. "Songs with Substance." *Words & Music,* Winter 2004: 12–14.

Kiener, Robert. "This Girl Just Wants to Rock." *Reader's Digest,* July 2004: 50–57.

Kimpel, Dan. "Avril Lavigne." *Music Connection,* 24 May 2004: 54–57.

Nathanson, Ian. "Avril Lavigne: When You're Canada's Biggest Starlet Life Is Complicated." *Chart,* October 2002: 36–40.

Interviews

Creighton, Lorraine. E-mail interview. 20 January 2006.

Jowett, Mark. Telephone interview. 16 January 2006.

King, Michelle. E-mail interview. 13 January 2006.

Lectures

McKillip, Tom. "It's Studio Time!" Music BC, Vancouver, BC. 11 February 2006.

Websites

avrilsux.tripod.com

music.aol.com

top40-charts.com

www.alavigne.com

www.amnesty.org

www.answers.com

www.at40.com

www.auralgasms.com

www.avrilbandaids.com

www.avrillavigne.com

www.bbc.co.uk

www.billboard.com

www.blender.com

www.bostonphoenix.com

www.canada.com

www.canoe.ca

www.cbc.ca

www.chartattack.com

www.comics.com

www.contactmusic.com

www.dickies.com

www.emimusicpub.com

www.evanworld.net

www.ew.com

www.garrisonequine.com

www.icmtalent.com

www.imdb.com

www.landmines.org

www.lennoxtheatre.ca

www.maximonline.com

www.mixguides.com

www.mnbc.msn.com

www.moono.com

www.msn.com

www.mtv.com

www.muchmusic.com

www.myplash.com

www.nytimes.com

www.popmatters.com

www.star-tv.com

www.stylusmagazine.com

www.theage.com.au

www.town.greaternapanee.on.ca

www.uscampaignforburma.org

www.vanmag.com

www.veg.ca

www.vh1.com

www.warchild.ca

www.wikipedia.org

www.wish.org

www.youthaids-aldo.org

Crystal Naka

NATASHA JAY

Natasha Jay is a singer-songwriter and classically trained flautist. Her love for music began at an early age when she took her first steps in her family's music school in Kelowna, BC. She went on to study music and French language at the University of British Columbia and completed her Bachelor of Arts in 2004. Natasha is also a former figure skater and has worked on several major events with some of the world's top skaters. Currently, Natasha is a freelance writer and professional musician and works in the field of community involvement and recreation in Vancouver, BC.

TRICKLE ROCK BOOKS

Real Canadians. Real stars.
The stories of Canada's music celebrities.

HOT CANADIAN BANDS

Steve MacLean
$9.95 • ISBN 10: 1-894864-53-0 • ISBN 13: 978-1-894864-53-4 • 5.25" x 8.25" • 144 pages

Canadian rock 'n' roll has exploded onto the North American and world music scene. Homegrown bands now play to packed stadiums coast to coast and top the music charts from London to Los Angeles. This book profiles some of the most exciting names in Canadian music:

- **Nickelback**, Canada's top-selling band and an international chart topper
- **Alexisonfire**, the unique post-hardcore "screamo" group that has a close personal connection to its fans
- **The Tragically Hip**, Canadian Music Hall of Fame inductee, has a rabid fan base and after 20 years on the road continues to draw people from all ages and backgrounds
- **Sum 41**, the group of brats who might be maturing after 10 years of performing but are still popular for their pop-punk sound
- **Simple Plan**, whose debut album was certified double platinum in Canada and the U.S.
- **Metric**, the female-fronted band that went from a slow burn to skyrocketing stardom
- **Arcade Fire**, the band that *Time* magazine says "helped put Canadian music on the world map" proves that indie music can steal the scene at home and around the globe
- **Broken Social Scene**, the eclectic musical collective that has spun off a variety of other hot acts and a trend-setting indie record label
- **Our Lady Peace**, the alternative rock group whose members work as hard for social causes as they do for their music.

And more...

Find Trickle Rock Books at your local bookseller and newsstand or contact the distributor, Lone Pine Publishing, directly. In the U.S. call 1-800-518-3541. In Canada, call 1-800-661-9017.